CASES IN
HOSPITALITY MANAGEMENT

CASES IN
HOSPITALITY MANAGEMENT
A Critical Incident Approach

Timothy R. Hinkin

Cornell University
School of Hotel Administration

JOHN WILEY & SONS, INC.

New York / Chichester / Brisbane / Toronto / Singapore

Library of Congress Cataloging-in-Publication Data:

Hinkin, Timothy R.
    Cases in hospitality management / Timothy R. Hinkin.
        p.   cm.
    Includes bibliographical references.
    ISBN 0-471-10754-9   (paper : acid-free paper)
    1. Hospitality industry—United States—Management—Case studies.
    I. Title.
    TX911.3.M27H56   1995
    647.94′068—dc20   94-39356

Printed in the United States of America
10 9 8 7 6 5 4

Preface

This book began when I started to look for short cases based on "real world" situations in the hospitality industry to use as an instructional tool in my own classes. The motive to develop my own cases was simple—there weren't any and I wanted some. With the help of students and colleagues, over 100 interviews have been conducted during the last several years with guests and employees of hospitality industry organizations. The methodology was straightforward: Interviewees were simply asked to describe an unpleasant occurrence that they had experienced either as a customer or as an employee, and to describe the organization's response to their situation. Interestingly, the people being interviewed could quickly and easily recall the events, and most of them had more than one from which to choose. Based on these interviews, the 55 short cases, or "critical incidents," in this book were created. Although names have been changed and a significant amount of editing has occurred, it is important to keep in mind that the premise of each incident is an event that actually happened.

The incidents have been selected because they are representative of situations students will face soon after entering the workplace. In understanding and analyzing these incidents, it is felt that students will become better prepared to manage relationships effectively with the external customers—the guests—and the internal customers—the employees.

The critical incident approach is used for a variety of reasons. First, very long and complex cases are often confusing to students and may obscure the importance of the human element in organizations. The critical incident approach adopts the "less is more" philosophy of education with an emphasis on depth rather than breadth of understanding. This approach encourages a thorough analysis of a prominent issue rather than a superficial analysis of a complicated case. Although at first glance these cases might appear to be relatively simple, an in-depth examination of the situations reveals the complexities inherent in even small, contained events, and allows the student to better understand the subtleties of human interaction often overlooked in lengthy cases. Second, these critical incidents provide a realistic context that accurately reflects scenarios in which students will soon find themselves. It is unlikely that recent graduates will be developing a major corporate strategic plan, but it is likely that they will have to deal with turnover, disgruntled guests, and demotivated employees. The level of analysis is appropriate as students will be given the opportunity to suggest how they would handle specific situations. In a sense, these incidents provide a realistic job preview of what is waiting for them just around the corner. Third, these incidents can easily be linked to course content to provide students the opportunity to practice their analytical and communication skills and to apply their substantive learning. Practice may not make perfect, but it is a good start. Fourth, critical incidents can be used to encourage students to think on their feet, as they can be included spontaneously in a course as deemed appropriate. Giving students 10 minutes of class time to read an incident and to prepare for discussion can result in an exciting classroom experience. Finally, critical incidents can be interesting, engaging, and fun. The truth, indeed, may be stranger than fiction, as some of the situations included in this book are almost unbelievable.

The incidents deal with a variety of managerial issues, such as decision making, communication, compensation, planning, discrimination, performance appraisal, organization design, sexual harassment, ethics, cultural differences, and group dynamics. It should be noted that there are no sections labeled "Leadership" or "Motivation," topics that typically get much attention in a book about management. This is not an oversight but is done intentionally. Issues of leadership and motivation are implicit in virtually every critical incident in this book, as they are in real life. It will be up to the students to identify and analyze these issues. The incidents include a lot of the "language of the industry" to familiarize them with the hospitality context. A number of segments of the hospitality industry are included, from airlines and travel agents to hotels and restaurants. There is also a major emphasis on service quality.

The book is organized into eleven parts, covering important issues in the hospitality industry. These parts were derived from content analyzing the interviews, and as such, the topics represent issues that are important to employees and guests of contemporary hospitality organizations. This structure allows the incidents to be presented in an orderly manner but certainly does not suggest that each issue is mutually exclusive or independent of the others. On the contrary, there is great opportunity to integrate the various issues to illustrate the complexity of organizations. For example, promotion practices may certainly affect group dynamics and decision making can severely affect motivation.

This book would be appropriate for use in introductory management, human resources management, organizational behavior, strategic management, or a course on total quality management. The Instructor's Manual will include the "what really happened" for many of the incidents, along with guidelines for class discussion. Hopefully, there will be many incidents appropriate for use in any course dealing with management in the hospitality industry.

I would like to offer my appreciation to my wife Linda for her help in selecting and editing the incidents and to the following people for contributing incidents to this book: Jeff Manheim, Roger Ahlfeld, Trond Bastian, Gretchen Bookbinder, Jennifer Chase, Rod Clough, Eileen Deghan, Jeremy Donaker, Yama Filipowicz, Debbie Freckleton, Benno Geruschkat, Brad Hudson, Ursula Kriegl, Jennifer Lai, Betsy McAffee, Derek McCann, Allison Morton, Jennifer Mosse, Vicki Pearl, J. Wade Pitts, Eric Rovner, Scott Seaman, Sue Snyder, BettyLou Tai, Themis J. Themistokleous, J. Bruce Tracey, Raynika J. Trent, Sharonda White, Leonard A. Whitehouse, Leo Yen, and Annette Zeller.

Contents

Contents

CASES IN
HOSPITALITY MANAGEMENT

Introduction

Organizations *are* the behavior of the people in them and the hospitality industry is a "people" business. It is perhaps the most labor intensive industry in the world and will probably continue to be so. Perhaps even more than in manufacturing industries, improvements in productivity and service quality must be made through better utilization of human resources. Unlike many other industries, graduates who enter the hospitality industry will quickly be assuming managerial roles. Helping to prepare you to be successful in those roles is the primary purpose of this book.

Today more than ever, organizations in the hospitality industry are faced with major challenges from both the external environment and the internal organizational context. Factors such as tightening economic conditions, a shrinking yet diverse labor force, an overbuilt real estate market, changing demographics, and downsizing have created demands on managers that simply did not exist a decade ago. Predictions for the next decade are quite optimistic but may exist largely in new markets and with new products and services. These conditions require extraordinary leaders who are able to transform their organizations to meet current and future challenges.

As managers you will be expected to establish the direction in which your organization will go. Regardless of whether you are managing a kitchen, a dining room, a front desk, a travel agency, a fast-food restaurant, or an entire hotel, your subordinates will be seeking cues and reinforcements from you to guide their behavior. You will need to recognize that you have both internal customers and external customers with a wide array of needs to be satisfied. The products and services that you offer must be driven by customer demand, and processes must be designed to add value to the guest or customer experience. Reward systems must be developed that encourage employees to strive to meet organizational objectives and progress toward reaching these objectives must be measured. You will need to create a working environment that fosters motivation, commitment, and continuous improvement.

This book will provide you with the opportunity to integrate the knowledge you are acquiring, to reflect back on your own experiences, and to hone your management skills. It will help you to understand organizations as the complex mosaics that they are. Although the names have been changed, the critical incidents in this book actually happened, and they are repeated in endless variations every day simply because managers are less competent than they need to be. By analyzing and understanding the causes and effects in these situations, you will be better prepared to deal effectively with similar situations when you face them, and you will. Managing will probably be the hardest thing you ever do, but it can also be the most rewarding of experiences. Remember, competence is your best defense.

You are now invited to delve into the magical, mystical, and mystifying world of the hospitality industry.

Part One

ETHICAL ISSUES: SHADES OF GRAY

It's important for people to know what you stand for. It's equally important that they know what you won't stand for.

—Unknown

It may seem a bit odd to place ethics in the beginning of a book about management. This was done for a reason. A large group of hospitality industry executives was recently asked "What skills and abilities do students need to obtain to be successful in the hospitality industry?" The executives rated approximately 50 items on a scale of 1 to 5 from not important to very important. The results of the survey may surprise you, and the top 10 responses are presented below.[1]

4.48 Ethics
4.25 Leadership
4.28 External Communication
4.23 Problem Identification
4.21 Organizing/Writing Skills
4.17 Motivating Others
4.16 Understanding the Big Picture
4.15 Decision Making

As you can see, ethics topped the list. It is not clear if this was because the executives were all very ethical and think it is important, or if they believe that ethical behavior is lacking in the industry and is needed. One thing is clear, however, ethical behavior is important, and all of you will be facing situations in which you will need to make difficult decisions that you will base on your ethical beliefs and value system.

Individual Ethics

Ethics is defined as "the system or code of morals of a particular person, religion, group, or profession."[2] As such, ethical beliefs may vary from person to person. Three basic individual approaches to ethics are reflected in the behavior of people. First is the moral rights approach, which judges the consistency of decisions and behaviors with the maintenance of certain fundamental personal and group liberties and privileges, such as life, freedom, health, privacy, and property. Second is the justice approach, which judges the consistency of decisions and behaviors with the maintenance of equity, fairness, and impartiality in the distribution of costs and benefits among individuals. Third is the utilitarian approach, which judges the effects of decisions and behaviors on providing the greatest good for the greatest number of people.

Business Ethics

Business ethics in Western society emerged with the growth of capitalism in sixteenth-century Europe. Up to that time it was largely believed that it was immoral to produce goods for profit. With the Protestant Reformation came the belief that a diligent worker pleased God and that the wealth that was acquired from business activities was a sign that God was pleased. Good businessmen could be good human beings by satisfying the needs of customers and providing employment for workers. Today there is a common belief among many organizations that good ethics is good business. This idea has evolved into the concept of social responsibility, and some companies, such as HVS and the Ecotel, have stressed the importance of energy conservation, recycling, and minimal disturbance of ecological systems in property development. It is too soon to tell if there is a positive relationship between social responsibility and profits, but there are clearly increasing numbers of companies who want to be known as being socially responsible. It is important to note that operating within the legal system may not be an adequate basis for evaluating the ethics of a business decision.[3]

Overview of the Incidents

The following incidents deal with several complex issues of both personal ethics and social responsibility that have occurred in hospitality organizations. In analyzing these incidents you should think about the relationship between ethics and the law. It should also become apparent to you which individual approach to ethics you favor.

Endnotes

[1]C. A. Enz, L. M. Renaghan, and A. N. Geller, "Graduate-Level Education: A Survey of Stakeholders," *Cornell Hotel and Restuarant Administration Quarterly*, August 1993, pp. 90–95.

[2]Discussion based on G. F. Cavanaugh, D. J. Mobery, and M. Velasquez, "The Ethics of Organizational Behavior," *Academy of Management Review*, Vol. 6, 1981, pp. 363–374.

[3]Discussion based on David Vogel, "Business Ethics Past and Present," *The Public Interest*, Vol. 102, 1991, pp. 49–84.

Case 1

Sunspot Resorts

Sunspot Resorts, Incorporated, is a publicly held international hotel firm that specializes in luxury resorts in exotic locations. Sunspot has in the last 20 years focused on oceanfront development all over the world in locations such as Greece, Cyprus, Mexico, Indonesia, Australia, and South America. They have opened three resorts in the Caribbean region over the last several years and are hoping to begin construction of another property in Barbados in the near future. Real estate negotiations for the purchase of a seafront location have stalled, however, due to complaints from environmental groups and local citizens. These groups are protesting because they feel that development will disrupt the fragile relationship of life on the reef that is immediately offshore. The environmentalists say they have seen many instances where developers destroyed pristine land and exploited native populations. They are determined not to let this happen in Barbados, and they have assembled the people and financial support to put up a major battle if necessary. The local residents have seen many changes in their island in the last several years. They are not totally opposed to development because it provides employment opportunities and tax revenues, but in the past, developers have made promises they have not kept and, as a result, many parts of the island have been ruined.

Sunspot has handled similar situations in the past by emphasizing the poor economic conditions in the host country and by promising jobs that will benefit the local community, even though they have often had difficulty providing these jobs. Sunspot management has found that the skill level of the local labor pool has typically been low and they have found it easier and less expensive to import most managerial and supervisory personnel from the United States or Europe rather than training the locals.

This time, however, the strategy does not seem to be working, and the local community is resisting Sunspot's advances in order to retain the pristine nature of the area. To date, several hundred thousand dollars have been invested in the planning and design of the resort at corporate headquarters in Seattle. The corporate president of Sunspot has made it clear that he wants a resort in this locale because of its unique environment and profit potential, and the annual bonus of the regional vice-president (RVP) is based on progress on the proposed development. The RVP has been in contact with the government of Barbados to push the economic perspective and has hired an attorney to attempt to portray the environmentalists as radical obstructionists.

Several local businessmen have approached him suggesting that they might know a way to overcome the resistance to the project, but they have implied that some sort of bribe might be necessary. Sunspot stock has recently gone up several points on the New York Stock Exchange based on anticipated profits from this highly publicized development that was presented enthusiastically in Sunspot's annual report and meeting, where it was announced that the opening would take place in 18 months.

1. What are the important issues in this situation?
2. Who are the primary customers of Sunspot?
3. What recommendations would you make to Sunspot management?

Case 2

The Hawaiian Village

Allison Webb was employed by the Hawaiian Village as the supervisor for all food and beverage cashiers. She thoroughly enjoyed her job and the working relationship she had with her employees. Ms. Webb directly supervised 45 cashiers and was expected to train these employees as well as the 29 bartenders who she supervised indirectly. She was also responsible for balancing all the cash drawers, programming the computers at all the food and beverage outlets, and depositing all revenues collected from her cashiers. Due to the largely financial nature of her job, Allison was supervised by the accounting department, not by the food and beverage department. Throughout the time she worked at the Hawaiian Village, she had been evaluated as a "good" to "excellent" employee. Allison had found her work environment to be excellent as well, except for two unfortunate incidents of sexual harassment, which she felt warranted the two separate grievances she had filed over the past 18 months.

In the summer approaching Allison's tenth year with the Village, it became necessary for her accounts clerk to question a cashier at the Seaside Hut, one of their beverage outlets, regarding a corporate account. This particular corporation had been extended a line of credit at the hotel, with its food and beverage transactions being recorded on vouchers. After defaulting on several payments, however, the corporation's credit was revoked by the accounting office and the cashier at the Seaside Hut was notified that "cash only" would be accepted for this account. Nonetheless, the accounts clerk had a voucher from the Seaside Hut showing credit sales to this corporate customer. The account clerk was trying to confirm that a mistake had been made in recording the sales on a credit voucher and that cash had actually been collected. The cashier did in fact remember collecting cash payments

9

for this particular customer and happened to mention to the account clerk that she had handed the money to the hostess for recording. The account clerk found this suspicious, and she notified Ms. Webb of the situation, drawing specific attention to the fact that the hostess had been in physical possession of the money. Further investigation by Allison revealed that the hostess at the Seaside Hut used her seniority to convince the cashier that she had permission to enter the cash drawer, record payments, and make deposits. The hostess also frequently complained to the cashier about her job, lamenting her low position and its lack of recognition. Responding to the norms of the work area and the hostess's negative attitude about her job, the cashier deferred to the hostess without really thinking beyond the cashier's immediate responsibilities of ringing up customer sales. Another problem Allison found was that the controller's office had set up a system without cross checks on the recording of payments and deposits. With no other employee required to verify these amounts, the hostess had complete autonomy to manipulate the Seaside Hut's ledger. The hostess had been recording cash payments of certain corporate customers as credit sales, using readily available vouchers, while pocketing the cash. Allison surmised that because the Seaside Hut was a relatively small outlet, the hostess assumed that its operation was dismissed by the accounting office as trivial and that her embezzlement would go undetected—which it had, for two years. In fact, if she had not written a credit voucher on an account that, unbeknownst to her, had been converted to "cash only," her theft might have continued.

Following this discovery, Allison promptly spoke to her immediate supervisor, Bill Tompkins. She felt that not only should disciplinary action be initiated but that the flaw in the system should be corrected as well. After obtaining all the information from Allison, Bill assured her that he would address the situation. Committed to her role as a supervisor, Allison wrote up the Seaside Hut cashier, citing her negligence in adhering to proper procedure. From their training, all cashiers knew that at no time were they to transfer cash to any person other than the appropriate accounting personnel.

The next week Allison went on vacation, pleased that it was her investigation that had revealed an inherent problem in the system and confident that Bill, working with the controller's office, would be able to correct it. Upon returning after a week's absence, she learned that the hostess and the manager of the outlet had been fired. Although feeling somewhat sorry for the Seaside Hut manager, Allison resumed her normal work with enthusiasm. At the end of her shift she was called to the office of the assistant controller, Harry Brunson, her supervisor's boss. Without any forewarning, Mr. Brunson terminated her, claiming that *she* was negligent in not having performed an audit of the outlet. Mr. Brunson claimed that the controller's office expected her to have done one as part of her routine job responsibilities. Allison left Harry's office in a state of shock and anger.

Later, at home that evening, she attempted to assess the whole situation. Sitting at her desk, she began to outline the events and the reasons for her termination. She did not believe the argument that she was actually expected to conduct an audit, as she was not a trained accountant. As supervisor of food and beverage cashiers, she doubted she would have had the authority to audit the Seaside Hut, which operated under the jurisdiction of the controller's office. Allison had not forgotten that it was procedures designed by the controller's office which had enabled the hostess to embezzle sales money, and later in the week she was to learn that except for the firing of the Seaside Hut manager and hostess, no action had been taken to correct the problem. Regarding audits, however, she decided that if in fact it was one of her responsibilities, it had not been made clear to her either by her supervisor, Bill, or in the job description of supervisor of food and beverage cashiers, which was vague and outdated. Allison concluded that there were two probable reasons why she was fired. One was that she was simply being used as a scapegoat to protect accountants in the controller's office, who were more than likely the ones responsible for running audits. The other was that her three male superiors saw her as a troublemaker in that she had revealed their inappropriately devised accounting procedure and had filed two sexual harassment grievances. Allison toyed with her pencil and considered filing charges against the Hawaiian Village for sexual discrimination and wrongful discharge.

1. How did this situation come about?
2. Was Allison at fault for any of the problems?
3. Who could have prevented this from happening? How?

Case 3

A Dog-Eat-Dog World

Jackie Luden had been working at the Kingswood Conference Center for almost two years. It was a wonderful place to work, as the facilities were state of the art and her fellow employees were extremely competent. Due to the nature of the conference center business she found that she worked primarily Monday through Friday, and seldom at night. She spent the first year of her employment in the front office training rotation and had become familiar with the operations of the front desk, reservations, and guest services. For the last nine months she had been working in the sales department and had reached a point where she was actively involved in developing and making presentations to potential clients. Her background in statistics and computers had prepared her particularly well for this new position.

She had spent the last several weeks doing research and preparing a presentation to the executive board of a medium-sized manufacturing firm. Kingswood was attempting to get this company to sign a multiyear contract to use their facility for their management development training programs. If successful, the contract would be worth several hundred thousand dollars. The presentation, however, did not go as Jackie had expected, and she had two major complaints. She felt that her work had not been well represented, first, in that she had not received credit for what she had done, and second, that Ericka, the sales manager who had actually made the presentation, had altered a lot of her material and falsified some information.

Several days after the presentation Jackie approached Ericka to discuss the situation. When Jackie entered Ericka's office she found that Ericka was exuberant about getting the account, and Ericka initiated their conversation by congratulating Jackie for her hard work. Although Ericka was excited and was attempting to make Jackie feel good about the success, this only made Jackie feel more uncomfortable about what she had to say. Ericka was surprised to learn that Jackie had come to see her about a problem and was even more surprised that the problem was about the new account.

Jackie began by asking why some of the information she had worked so hard on researching had either been changed or left out of the presentation entirely. Ericka responded by asking, "We wanted to get the account, didn't we?" This made Jackie very uneasy, since in a discussion prior to the presentation Ericka had assured her that everything in Jackie's report was perfect and that no changes were necessary. Jackie said that she felt it was dishonest to the customer to falsify information, but Ericka reverted to her previous argument that her actions were in the best interest of the company. Ericka did not understand Jackie's disappointment because they had gotten the account, and replied simply, "It's a dog-eat-dog world out there."

As Ericka continued to praise Jackie for all the hard work she had done, Jackie felt that this was an opportune time to question her about the lack of credit she received at the presentation. Ericka explained that she did not get the recognition because she was her subordinate, saying "It simply doesn't work that way." She informed Jackie that the higher she gets in the company hierarchy, the more credit she will get, no matter who does the work.

Still annoyed by the situation, Jackie requested that any changes or "falsifications" in her work not be made in the future or, at least, if they were that she would like to be informed. She told Ericka that she would feel better if she was able to expect them rather than have them surprise her, and asked if they could meet prior to the next presentation to go over the material. Although Ericka noted that "falsifications" was much too strong a word, she agreed to meet and notify Jackie of any changes the day before the next presentation.

1. Who is right in this situation?
2. How often do you think this type of incident occurs?
3. What would you do if you were Jackie?
4. What are some of the possible costs involved?

Case 4

The Second Honeymoon

The McDonalds are a couple in their late fifties who decided to return to Hawaii for their second honeymoon. Although they had liked the hotel in which they had stayed in the past, they decided that they would try a different one, the Waikiki Palace, which was highly recommended by their travel agent. Mr. McDonald had also briefly visited this hotel previously while on a business trip to Hawaii, and he thought it was a beautiful location to celebrate their anniversary.

Arriving at the island airport early in the evening they expected to be met by a limousine from the hotel, but after it failed to appear in 20 minutes, they called a taxi. When they entered the hotel, they found that it was undergoing a major renovation, a detail that had not been mentioned by the travel agent. Their check-in went smoothly and the front desk clerk remarked that she hoped the renovations would not inconvenience them in any way, but neglected to mention in what ways guest services were affected. The bellman courteously escorted them to their suite, carefully placed their luggage in the room, dismissed the renovations as not being troublesome, and wished them a pleasant stay. They enjoyed a late dinner on the terrace overlooking the ocean and later, sipping on tropical drinks, they toasted their decision to return to Hawaii.

The next morning the McDonalds indulged in a leisurely breakfast, changed into swimwear, and went down to the olympic-size pool to relax and unwind. Shortly after settling into their chaise lounges, they were startled by the sound of pneumatic drills and heavy machinery coming from across the swimming pool. It was a beautiful day and they hoped that the noise would soon stop. After enduring the disturbing construction rumble for 30 minutes, they were preparing to leave when the drilling ceased. Relieved, Mrs. McDonald resumed her seat while

Mr. McDonald went to get a cup of coffee at the poolside cafe. He found it closed due to the renovation, posted with a sign stating that he could buy food and refreshments in the coffee shop inside the hotel. As he made his way through the lobby toward the restaurant, he was stopped by a manager and informed that proper attire was required in all common areas inside the hotel. In the exchange that followed, Mr. McDonald learned that he was expected to get fully dressed to go into the hotel to get a cup of coffee or to visit the rest room. As an alternative, the manager suggested that he could order from room service, but further discussion with the manager revealed that there was a minimum charge of $15, even under the unusual circumstances of the outside cafe being closed, which Mr. McDonald was unwilling to pay.

Disgruntled, Mr. McDonald requested to see a senior manager. He waited for over 20 minutes and was eventually addressed by a front desk clerk. After a brief discussion the clerk informed Mr. McDonald that she could do nothing about the situation but she would get her supervisor. Finally, he was met by an assistant manager, who apologized profusely and later a complimentary bottle of champagne was delivered to the suite.

The next day presented all of the same disturbances, encounters, and complaints, with the addition of a rain shower during which all of the pool cushions were removed from the chairs. When the skies cleared, Mrs. McDonald requested two cushions from the poolman and was refused, being told "It might rain again." Once again Mr. McDonald went into the hotel and proceeded directly to the hotel's executive offices in his bathing suit and a tee shirt. After waiting for 10 minutes, he was introduced to the hotel's general manager, who listened while Mr. McDonald described all of the problems that had occurred during their stay. The general manager apologized and that evening another complimentary bottle of wine was sent to the suite. Mr. and Mrs. McDonald found it extremely upsetting to think that the hotel intended merely to assuage their complaints with gifts rather than correct the problems.

The following morning Mr. McDonald again went to the general manager and made it clear that if he wanted a bottle of wine or champagne that he was more than capable of buying it for himself. He informed the GM that it was of far more importance to him that the events of the previous days were not repeated and they could receive a cup of coffee in peace and quiet at the pool. The GM assured them that this would be the case for the rest of their stay and that room service would provide them with whatever they requested at the swimming pool. Later that morning when he requested coffee from room service he was told that there was a $15 minumum charge.

1. Why is the McDonald's vacation turning out so poorly?
2. What effect did their expectations have on the incident?
3. How did the behavior of the GM help or hinder the situation?
4. Can anything be done to resolve the situation?

Case 5

Seaside Plantations

Liza Slater was a property manager with over 10 years of experience specializing in resorts and 20 years in the hospitality industry. She had previously been the director of property management for Seaside Plantations, a beach resort located on Bayside Island that catered to both families and convention business. In this position, Liza was responsible for the communication between the resort operating company and the individual owners of the condominiums on Seaside Plantation's rental program. Liza had been in this position for five years and had developed a good working relationship of trust and mutual respect with the condominium owners. She left this position due to her family and their growing needs.

Two years later a powerful storm struck the island and nearly destroyed Seaside Plantations. Liza felt a responsibility to return to the resort to help the property owners, who had experienced great losses, both economic and emotional. Since most of the condominium owners lived in other, distant locations, they desperately needed an agent on the island to help them through the reconstruction period and to prepare their villas again for rental. Time was of the essence, as most property owners had suffered enormous loss of rental income due to the storm.

The original property management company for whom Liza had worked had offices and front desk check-in on the premises. This company closed, however, after the storm and was eventually sold to a new company, Condominiums, Inc., which then occupied the vacated space. In the meantime, Liza accepted a position with a competitor, Oaks Properties, a prominent resort rental company. Oaks Properties owned and operated two other villa resort rental programs in the area and had just purchased a villa rental company on Bayside Island, three miles from Seaside Plantations. Since Oaks Properties did not have previous rental experience on this island, they were particularly interested in hiring Liza because she was so familiar with the Seaside Plantations property, the property owners, and their condominiums. Liza's responsibilities included the day-to-day supervision of the office, including reservations, front desk activities, and property management functions, as well as overseeing both the housekeeping and maintenance operations. Although she lived at the resort, Lisa had to travel the three miles to the office and was on call seven days a week, 24 hours a day.

Marketing was handled exclusively by the home office located on another island. The owners of Oaks Properties had decided to compete aggressively on Bayside Island in an effort to increase their market share in both reservations and number of villas in their Seaside Plantations rental program. They used the Seaside Plantations name throughout all of the advertising without specifically identifying themselves as Oaks Properties, a rental/property management agency for the resort. This strategy was carried into their brochures, telephone advertising, and conference sales. Prospective guests assumed that they were reaching the on-site reservations office for Seaside Plantations rather than a separately located rental agency. Callers thought that they were making reservations directly with Seaside Plantations and that their stay would include certain amenities of the resort. Bookings made through the competing on-site property management company, Condominium, Inc., for instance, offered golf and tennis privileges at reduced rates, a free summer children's program, free transportation within Seaside Plantations, and convenient charging privileges at the front desk for all food and clothing outlets. Although Oaks Properties offered slightly lower rental rates, their check-in desk was located three miles from the front gate of the resort, they did not offer special amenities, they required the full payment for the accommodations within two weeks of booking the reservation, and it was nonrefundable 14 days prior to arrival. While Liza did not approve of Oaks Properties' strategy, she initially had some ability to correct the misperceptions of potential guests by instructing her reservations staff to provide complete information to the guest when they were inquiring or booking reservations.

During the second year of operations, Oaks Properties' management decided that the three reservation offices located on separate islands should be consolidated, and the reservation function was moved to the main office. By making this move the satellite operating office that Liza managed no longer had control over the information that was given to the prospective guest prior to making the reservation. Management also decided that the staff should be cut in half on Bayside Island since this office no longer handled reservations. This did not allow for sufficient staff to handle the problems of the property owners or guest services.

Difficulties for Liza and her staff began soon after this consolidation. Oaks Properties invested heavily in marketing their properties. All types of advertising had the name "Seaside Plantations" prominently displayed, with only a small lettered notation of "Oaks Properties" and the address. The reservations office, now under control of the home office, answered the telephone "Seaside Plantations Reservations," not Oaks Properties. The 800 directory listed "Seaside Plantations Accommodations," but in reality was the 800 number for Oaks Properties.

The change caused a great deal of confusion for guests, particularly for check-in procedures. Since many of the guests did not realize they were renting through Oaks Properties they would go to the main resort front desk, run by Condominiums, Inc., where they would be directed to the Oaks Properties office, three miles away, to check in. During the busy summer months it was not unusual for guests to creep slowly along in congested traffic to reach Seaside Plantations, where they would then wait at the front desk only to be sent back the three miles. Often, the delay caused by the check-in confusion would be over 45 minutes and was typically endured in subtropical heat. Many had small children in the car and had been traveling for several hours. By the time the guests finally arrived at Oaks Properties to check-in, they were hot, tired, and terribly irritated.

Oaks Properties policies gave Liza and her staff no way to appease these guests. They could merely point out that no misrepresentation had occurred since the name and address of Oaks Properties did appear on the brochure and reservation confirmation. The only positive information they could provide was that Oaks Properties rental rates were slightly lower than those of Condominiums, Inc. In addition, since the deposit was now nonrefundable, guests would forfeit their money if they did not keep their reservation.

Although this was an extremely upsetting situation for Liza and her staff, there were other equally distressing occurrences. Oaks Properties did not operate their Bayside Island office, including the front desk, on a 24-hour basis. When the office closed at 8 P.M., check-in information was left in a box for the guest to pick up. Guests arriving late at night, most having gone directly to the resort first, were greeted by a rental packet and key when they returned to Oaks Properties. Often, the security office or the front desk of Seaside Plantations would call Liza at home to handle an irate guest. On these occasions, she was forced to leave her two children unattended, sometimes after midnight, to unlock the door of a condominium, while trying to calm the guest. Even if the staff and Liza survived the check-in, there were other troubles. Included in the summer rates charged by Condominium, Inc., at Seaside Plantations was a free all-day children's program. Many families visited the resort during the summer and this was an important amenity. A sign was prominently displayed on the main road by the resort that read "registration for the children's program." Although the program was available only to guests who booked through Condominium, Inc., all guests driving to their accommodations could not fail to see this sign. Guests who had made their reservations through Oaks Properties would often try to register their children in the program only to be told that they could not. Once again Liza and her staff had very angry guests on their hands, and once again they could only point out that they paid a lower rate for the accommodations through Oaks Properties.

In addition to Liza's misgivings regarding the marketing and management practices of Oaks Properties, their compensation policy further complicated her predicament. Liza was paid a base salary that no longer met her financial needs. The company had eliminated any base salary increases and had decided instead that any additional compensation would be received in the form of a bonus for performance. Part of the bonus they paid Liza was based on how much she "comped" guests to appease them. Although Liza often felt that a guest was entitled to some recompension, the less Liza gave away in the form of complimentary gifts or services, the more she received for her bonus. She was also paid a very large fee every time she obtained a new rental unit for Oaks Properties. This put her in the position of having to be aggressive in securing villas for their rental program, when she did not personally feel their operating methods were ethical.

Liza's integrity and values were very important to her, but as a single parent she felt she had no alternative except to do her best for Oaks Properties until another comparable position could be found. She was also bound to Oaks Properties by her sense of fairness. Although she had been approached by several direct competitors, she did not think joining their organizations would be appropriate. Once again, the end came when Liza put her family's needs first. She realized that not only was she suffering from the stress of her job but that her children were as well. The ethical dilemmas she faced every day left her emotionally drained. The long hours she worked, with little or no opportunity to leave the island as she was to be on call around the clock, left her physically exhausted. She had for some time been unavailable to give her children the attention they needed.

1. Evaluate the strategy of Oaks Properties.
2. What impact did the strategy have on internal customers?
3. What could Liza have done in this situation?
4. Make a prediction about the future of Oaks Properties.

Case 6

The Rental Car

Mr. and Mrs. Rowan had extensive travel experience both in the United States and abroad. They had visited the former Soviet Union, Poland, Mexico, South America, South Africa, Europe, Southeast Asia, and China. Through their travels, the couple learned many strategies for avoiding the theft of their belongings, acts of violence, and being taken advantage of by local merchants and businesses.

Despite numerous warnings from their travel agent and friends, the couple traveled to Costa Rica with the belief that their previous experience as travelers would assist them in avoiding the pitfalls and complications that often plagued visitors to this country. Their trip began in March and lasted almost three weeks. Their itinerary was fairly unstructured, as they did not intend to travel with any tour groups or trip guides. The basic plan was to visit a family friend in San José, Costa Rica, and then to tour the country by rental car for the duration of their stay.

The trip to Costa Rica turned out to be a complete success. After an excellent visit with their friends, the Rowans drove to the many cities and destinations that were recommended by travel agents, friends, and other tourists. They had wonderful experiences with the local people they met and were very satisfied with the lodging and dining facilities they patronized. The weather had been perfect, and they found the natural beauty of the country almost overwhelming. During the three weeks, they drove almost 2000 miles without any problems either with the car or with local law enforcement officials.

On their flight back to the United States, the Rowans discussed how pleasant the trip had been and how strange it was that they had not encountered many of the challenges described by friends and their travel agent. They decided that the success of their trip was due to a combination of luck and their well-developed travel skills. Unfortunately, one of the major transactions that occurred on the trip would come back to haunt them long after their return home.

The principal means of transportation while in Costa Rica was the rental car. Based upon advice from travel agent, the couple rented their car from a well-established, U.S.-based rental car company to assure that they would have reliable transportation and service. They used one of their major credit cards to pay for the rental. Their confidence in the rental company was reaffirmed when their flat tire was quickly serviced on the ninth day of their visit.

At the end of the trip, the Rowans checked out of their hotel very early and left the car in the airport drop-off at 6:00 A.M. in order to catch their 7:30 flight. The rental car company did not perform a final inspection of the vehicle when it was returned because their hours of operation were from 8:00 A.M. to 6:00 P.M.

Almost three months after they had returned to the United States, the Rowans received a credit card statement that included a bill from the rental car company that exceeded what they owed by $2038. They quickly contacted their credit card company to investigate the overcharge and were told that the extra amount was to pay for damages they inflicted upon the rental car. When they told the credit card company representative that they had not caused any damage to the car, they were instructed to write letters to both the auto rental company and the credit card company explaining the situation. They quickly followed these instructions and waited anxiously for a response to their letters.

Three weeks later, the couple received a letter from the credit card company stating that it was their policy to cover the $2038 bill if the customers had contested the charges in good faith. The Rowans immediately called the credit card company, explained that they had contested in good faith, and were told that they would receive credit for the contested charge. After breathing a sigh of relief, the Rowans questioned the credit card representative about the frequency with which such events occur. He explained that these types of problems happen only occasionally and are usually associated with rental car agencies in certain countries. Further questioning revealed that the credit card company would pay the charge because it was cheaper than fighting with the rental car agency.

1. What could have been done to prevent this situation?
2. Should the credit card company just accept this situation?
3. Who will ultimately pay for this type of practice?

Part Two

STRATEGIC PLANNING

*Many of the problems that exist in organizations
are the result of the way products and processes
were designed. In a sense, management planned it
that way.*

—J. M. JURAN[1]

It is said that people don't plan to fail, they fail to plan. In his book *Planning for Quality*, J. M. Juran discusses the difference between the American and Japanese methods of bringing new products or services to the marketplace. This is illustrated in the following figure:

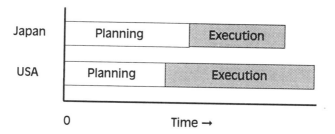

As the graph reveals, if more time is spent on the front end, products and services could be developed more quickly. We have a tendency to want to jump into action, however, because we believe we don't have time to plan. Planning is a major responsibility for managers in the hospitality industry, yet many of them complain that they don't have time to plan because they are too busy "fighting fires." The question might be asked: Why is there so much emphasis on fighting fires and so little emphasis on fire prevention?

The Strategic Planning Process

There are three primary stages in the strategic planning process. First, a manager must define the objective—where the organization wants to go. Second, the manager must identify where the organization is, both internally and externally. Third, the manager must decide how to get to the objective. These steps are elaborated upon below.

STEP 1: DEFINING THE OBJECTIVE

An effective manager must have a vision of what the organization can be. This vision must be articulated and communicated through the development of a mission statement, strategy, tactics, and finally, through the implementation of individual tasks. The focus of this planning process must be on meeting customer expectations, as the degree to which these expectations are met will determine success or failure. The tone of the organization is set at the top. The strategy then cascades down through the organization and becomes translated into specific behaviors at each level. Objectives must be specific, measurable, achievable, accepted, and clearly understood.

STEP 2: ENVIRONMENTAL ANALYSIS

Perhaps the most useful means of assessing the organizational environment is the SWOT (strengths, weaknesses, opportunities, threats) analysis. This first requires an examination of internal strengths and weaknesses such as staffing, technology, and training and requires the recognition of organizational constraints and obstacles. For example, inadequate training may prevent an organization from attaining its objectives. This is accompanied by the examination of opportunities and threats that may exist outside the organization, such as customers, suppliers, competitors, and regulatory agencies. Organizations do not exist in a vacuum, and overlooking the needs of customers in developing a new product or service may result in disaster.

STEP 3: STRATEGY FORMULATION AND IMPLEMENTATION

Once the management has a clear sense of objectives and an understanding of the internal and external environment, a specific plan must be developed to achieve the objective. At this stage products and processes must be designed to meet the needs of the organization. In striving to achieve objectives, organizations must both be efficient, maximizing the utilization of resources, and effective, meeting the demands of customers and guests.

Overview of the Incidents

Most of you will not be developing corporate strategies in the near future as this is typically done by top-level executives, but it is important that you understand the process and the importance of a clear strategy to individuals throughout the organization. The following incidents illustrate how planning, or lack thereof, has led to both undesired and unexpected outcomes in hospitality organizations.

Endnote

[1]J. M. Juran, *Juran on Quality by Design*. New York: Free Press, 1992.

Case 7

The New Consultant

Jeff Stewart had spent his summers during high school working at a large resort not far from his home in Florida. Upon graduation, he began his university studies in hospitality management. During the following three summers he worked in a number of different restaurants. Specializing in food and beverage management, Jeff graduated with honors from the four-year program and eagerly accepted an offer to join in the startup of Will Walker and Associates (W&A), a hospitality management consulting and training firm.

Jeff was second in command of the then two-person operation. Will Walker was a very charismatic person who had spent many years in the hospitality industry, specializing in restaurant franchising. He had established contacts with two major national restaurant chains and was in the process of negotiating multiyear contracts for developing customized training programs. Mr. Walker hired Jeff because of his education, experience, and enthusiasm, along with the fact that they were both alumni of the same university. Due to W&A's success with their two primary clients and the resulting word-of-mouth advertising, the company grew rapidly for the three years since Jeff joined the firm. In the last six months Mr. Walker had hired two new consultants who had begun to work with several new clients. W&A had more business than they could handle, and Mr. Walker was reveling in his success.

Due to the small size of W&A, the operational style had been quite casual. The organization had a nearly flat management structure with only five people. There was no mission statement, no set goal, and no plan of action. Mr. Walker did not want to limit the scope of the business. This lack of specific direction, however, caused the organization to suffer, specifically in the overextension of its resources in taking on a large number of diverse projects. The work environment, although rewarding, was frenzied and stressful. The consultants spent a major portion of their time traveling and worked very long hours. They had little administrative support, as there was only one administrative aide in the home office in New York, and this aide was typically inexperienced, due to chronic turnover in the position. In the absence of specific working plans for the junior consultants, Mr. Walker was forced to ask a continual barrage of questions of each of them as to what they were doing and why they were doing it. Mr. Walker required that the consultants contact him by telephone every day when they were working with a client, which was often very difficult to do. Recently, some important projects did not go as planned and outside deadlines were missed, further increasing the tension and frustration at W&A.

Jeff, tired of operating on a day-to-day basis with no clear plans or objectives, approached Mr. Walker with the suggestion that they start holding regular meetings to establish priorities, create plans, and assess performance. Since Jeff had been with the organization from the start and worked side by side with the owner, he felt within reason to make such a request. Mr. Walker sighed in agreement and said that as soon as they had time, they would organize such a meeting to talk about "Jeff's plan." Although initially pleased, Jeff was disappointed when such a meeting was never arranged. From Jeff's perspective, W&A remains overextended, committed to too many different projects, some of which venture beyond the scope of the company's expertise. In contrast, Mr. Walker feels the company thrives operating at its outside limits and that planning time is nonproductive.

1. Evaluate Mr. Walker's strategy.
2. How would you feel working in this type of environment?
3. What are some of the potential costs of this type of operation?
4. What prediction might you make about Jeff's future?

Case 8

The Tarragassett Inn

The Tarragassett Inn is a 100-room hotel located near a major ski area in northern Maine. Hotels in the area often are full on weekends during the winter. When Mr. and Mrs. Blain arrived at the Tarragassett Inn at 12:15 P.M. on a February Friday, they were told that they would have to wait to check in, as all of the rooms were not yet cleaned. The front desk clerk told them that the inn was short two housekeepers and the rooms would not be ready until 4:30. Although at first upset, the Blains were quickly pacified when the clerk gave them each a complimentary afternoon ski pass. The Blains were actually quite impressed by the fine service that they had received as they made their way to the slopes.

When they arrived back at the inn to check in at 4:30 P.M. they were met with a big surprise. The front desk clerk, a different one from the one they had dealt with earlier, informed them that the hotel was overbooked and they would have to find other accommodations for the night. At first, Mr. Blain was not fazed because he thought that the desk clerk had simply made a mistake. He showed her his reservation confirmation card and told her that he had tried to check in earlier and that the morning clerk told him he would have to check in later. The front desk clerk apologized to Mr. Blain and explained that she was not mistaken. The Inn had overbooked by approximately 10 percent and unfortunately for Mr. and Mrs. Blain, they had been bumped.

Mr. Blain then questioned why he was not told about this when he tried to check in at noon. The clerk then explained to him that the Tarragassett Inn's policy is to give ski passes to the overbooked guests and tell them to check in at 4:30. They do not tell the guest that there is a possibility that they might be bumped. If the other guests of the inn have not checked in by 4:00, the inn starts giving the rooms to the bumped guests. The inn's logic for this plan is simple. On average, 10 percent of their reservations cancel at the last minute or do not show up because of weather conditions. Thus, if the inn overbooks by 10 percent and 10 percent of the guests with reservations do not show up, the inn still has 100 percent occupancy. They determine which guests to bump by using a set criterion. Guests whom have not previously stayed at the inn, and/or do not live in New England, are the first to be bumped. Management believes that these guests are dispensable because they probably would not turn into frequent guests of the hotel.

Mr. Blain accepted the weak rationale, but he still wanted to know why they were not honest with him when he had tried to check in. If he knew there was a possibility that he was not going to be able to have a room, he would have gone to another hotel. At that point the clerk laughed and told Mr. Blain that he had answered his own question. If the morning clerk had been honest with Mr. Blain and told him that he had been bumped, he would have looked elsewhere for a room. Had Mr. Blain done that, the inn's reservation plan would not have worked. Mr. and Mrs. Blain had to drive over 30 miles that night to find alternative accommodations.

When Mr. Blain returned home he wrote letters to numerous agencies associated with the Tarragassett Inn, including AAA, Maine Inn Keeper's Association, Better Business Bureau, Maine Travel and Tourism Association, and even the governor of the state of Maine. He also wrote to the owners, management, and employees of the Tarragassett Inn to express his discontent with his experience. Although these responses were damaging to the inn, their effects were minimal compared to Mr. Blain's other action. Mr. Blain, who is a senior vice-president at Citibank, travels the East Coast lecturing on business strategy. As part of his presentation, he often tells the Tarragassett Inn story to a group of executives to whom he is lecturing. To this day, he estimates that he has told the story to at least 3000 people.

1. What effect did this policy have on external customers?
2. What effect did this policy have on internal customers?
3. What predictions might you make about the future of the inn?

CASE 9

The Cedars

The Cedars is a 300-room luxury seaside resort in a relatively remote area on the coast of the Adriatic Sea. It has for many years maintained the reputation of providing not only deluxe accommodations but superior service from both management and staff. The majority of the employees lived close by and had been hired in the years following World War II. These employees felt that they had been well taken care of over the years and that loyalty to the organization was very high. As a result, turnover has historically been very low, especially when compared to industry averages.

In the last several years, many of these long-time employees have begun to retire. The labor pool in the small town has diminished over the years as more and more people have moved to the larger cities to seek employment. As a result, retiring employees have been replaced by young men and women from the surrounding area, who often have to travel several miles to get to work.

In the past few years the quality of service at the Cedars has deteriorated severely, although the building and grounds have continued to be well cared for and the quality of food, linens, entertainment, and other amenities has been maintained. The resort is beginning to lose some of its long-time repeat customers, and the reputation of the Cedars is felt to be threatened. The general manager has met with his executive staff, who believe that control systems are breaking down and supervisory personnel need to exert more authority over low-level employees. The more senior employees seem to believe that the younger workers are irresponsible and lazy and resist authority. The newer employees believe that they have some ideas that might help the resort, but that no one listens to their opinions.

The general manager was hired nine months ago to replace the former manager who retired after being at the property for 11 years. The owners had hoped that the new manager would be able to turn the situation around, but after the better part of a year they have seen little evidence of progress. The owners are planning a meeting with the general manager and his staff to attempt to prescribe a course of action to get the resort pointed in the right direction.

1. What is wrong with the Cedars?
2. Where should the general manager focus his attention?
3. Develop an action plan to assist the manager.

Case 10

The ICO Conference

Professor Markham, the president of the International Communications Organization, was preparing for the group's annual conference, which was to take place in two and a half years. Since well over 500 participants were expected, planning several years in advance was imperative to secure the conference and guestroom space that they would need. Professor Markham contacted Riverview, a convention hotel in Memphis, Tennessee, and negotiated an acceptable price for the member's three-day conference. As part of the contract, the hotel promised Professor Markham complimentary accommodations in the Mississippi suite, since she was the president of the organization and would be hosting a small reception for the executive committee of the association.

Two years later, Riverview was sold to a private hotel chain. Five months prior to hosting the convention, Professor Markham was notified by letter of the ownership change and instructed that although the space was still reserved, the contract would have to be renegotiated. The new owners of the property refused to transfer directly any of the contracts made with the original sales office, as they felt that the rates quoted previously would not be profitable to the hotel.

Professor Markham, realizing that she had no feasible alternatives at this late date, was forced to negotiate a different contract with the new owners. The contract was more costly than the agreement with the previous management company, yet the Mississippi Suite was still offered as a token of appreciation. Professor Markham was forced to write a letter notifying all association members of the increased cost for attending the conference and to apologize for any inconvenience this might cause. Although she explained the reason for the increase and the inability to obtain another location, she felt that the situation would still reflect quite negatively on her. As she expected, many members telephoned her to complain. Several had already had their travel budgets approved and may not be able to obtain the additional money that was now needed. Others were indignant about the hotel's breech of contract and chose to cancel their plans to attend the conference.

On Friday afternoon, the day the conference was to begin, Professor Markham arrived to prepare for the reception that was to take place several hours later in the Mississippi Suite. When the Professor went to register at the front desk the clerk replied, "We have no clean rooms at this time." Realizing that the reception needed to be organized in less than three hours, Professor Markham told the clerk in an authoritative tone who she was and which suite was supposed to be hers for the weekend. The clerk, who was becoming annoyed with the Professor's insistence, responded coldly, "We have no clean rooms. Come back in a couple of hours." Her patience tested, Professor Markham demanded to speak with the front desk manager, and once again explained the situation. The manager only repeated the clerk's litany, adding: "You can leave your luggage in the storage room and we can get a single room cleaned for you in a few hours."

Thoroughly annoyed with the incompetency of the front desk, Professor Markham sought to resolve the problem through the sales department. One of the managers in the sales office realized the hotel's mistake, but that did not alter the fact that the Mississippi Suite was indeed not clean or ready for service. In an effort to facilitate Professor Markham's preparation for the function, the sales manager decided to send a maid to clean the living and dining room of the suite, as the reception was to be held in these common areas.

As the time of the reception approached, only the keys to the common areas had been given to the professor because the bedroom of the suite had not been cleaned. The people from the food and beverage department arrived on time and did an adequate job serving drinks and hors d'oeuvres to the executive committee. Several people complained to Professor Markham about their check-in experience, however, as the lines were long, service was slow, and the lobby congested. Several remarked that it seemed as if the front desk was unaware that a large group from the association was arriving that day.

As an organizer of the conference, Professor Markham felt responsible for the situation, and again sensed that this failure on the part of the hotel reflected negatively on her.

It was not until late that night that the bedroom area of the suite was cleaned. No apology was given nor was any extra effort made by the hotel staff to ensure the comfort of the professor.

1. Was the contract renegotiation appropriate?
2. Why were there so many service deficiencies?
3. What are some of the potential costs of this incident?

Case 11

The Broadbeach

The Broadbeach Resort Hotel is part of an international corporation of luxury hotels. It is located on the small island of St. John in the U.S. Virgin Islands. Since the island does not have an airport, guests to the island fly into the airport on nearby St. Thomas and reach St. John by ferry or helicopter. The Broadbeach property is over 30 acres, and the hotel facilities are spread among 13 separate structures built on the shallow side of a hill. The front desk is located at the highest point of the property, farthest away from the beach and the ferry dock. Most guests choose to take the ferry that operates between the two islands.

The Broadbeach Resort Hotel has a representative stationed at a desk in the St. Thomas airport terminal. Guests usually have instructions from their travel agents or from the reservation clerk at the hotel directing them to sign in at the airport desk. Guests are then driven 45 minutes across the island of St. Thomas in an open-air van to the ferry dock, where they wait for a large boat to complete their journey to St. John. The ferry travels on an hourly schedule, so the guests sometimes wait 20 or 30 minutes for the ride. The boat trip lasts approximately 20 minutes. Immediately after the van leaves for the ferry dock, the representative at the airport alerts the hotel as to which guests will be arriving on the boat. This allows the front desk clerks at the Broadbeach property ample time to collect the necessary registration packets from their office and take them down to the dock, where they quickly check guests in, provide them with room keys, and usher them to their rooms. The system is well received, as it saves guests from walking up the hill to the front desk.

On any particular day, the Broadbeach will have guests checking into up to 50 rooms. Occasionally, guests who land at the airport do not check in at the hotel's desk in the terminal. It is assumed by the hotel that the guests either did not see it or that the representative had momentarily stepped away from the desk. Having no notice of their arrival, when these guests dock at the hotel, their registration packets are not immediately available and they are forced to wait an additional 15 to 20 minutes while the front desk staff retrieves the registration materials and room keys.

On a certain Saturday, usually a particularly busy day for arrivals, Mr. and Mrs. Martin were landing at the airport on St. Thomas. Their ultimate destination was the Broadbeach Resort Hotel on St. John. They did not check in at the hotel desk, but instead saw the Broadbeach van and boarded it for the trip to the ferry dock. The van waited in the airport for about 15 minutes to collect all the hotel passengers before departing. After the 45-minute trip across St. Thomas, the van arrived at the ferry dock. The guests then waited another 10 minutes before they could board the ferry that would transport them and their luggage to the hotel. After the 20-minute ferry ride, the boat pulled into the dock at the Broadbeach, where the front-desk manager, Juan, greeted the guests with glasses of rum punch and directed them to the registration desk 50 feet away for their check-in. In the middle of the line stood the Martins, unaware that they were not expected on this particular boat. When they reached the front of the line, the registration clerk discovered that their packet was not among the others, and she left to retrieve it from the front desk office.

The Martins were understandably upset. Since landing in St. Thomas, they had spent 90 minutes traveling to get to the hotel and were now expected to wait another 15 minutes for their room. Like most of the other arriving guests, the Martins were from the East Coast of the United States, and were dressed for temperatures in the low forties, not the low nineties typical of St. John. Hot and tired, they complained to the front desk manager that the situation was intolerable. Juan had often dealt with similarly annoyed guests, and he apologized for the oversight. He explained to Mr. and Mrs. Martin about the airport sign-in process and said that he was terribly sorry that they had "slipped through" the system. The Martins were not satisfied with a simple apology and continued to voice their displeasure about the lack of service and the frustration of a travel-filled day. Juan graciously promised to send the Martins a bottle of wine and a fruit plate for their inconvenience.

The Martins were particularly irritated by the incident because of their expectations of the hotel chain with which the Broadbeach Resort was affiliated. They had often stayed at other hotels in the corporation and had come to expect a high standard of service. The corporation is known as one that provides the "extras" for its guests. No request is considered unreasonable by the staff, and every effort is supposed to be made to ensure the guest's total satisfaction.

At the Broadbeach Resort, front-line managers such as Juan are allowed to make decisions regarding guest complaints, to the extent that they are instructed to make quick amends to dissatisfied guests so as to avoid having guest complaints communicated to the corporate office. Upper management at the Broadbeach also relies on the expectation that if a guest does have a problem during the week, even if the problem is significant, the guest will have found the stay overall to be so delightful that a single incident is minimized by the time he or she checks out. Based on this philosophy, Juan believed that simply providing a complimentary gift was the appropriate action and one that would sufficiently appease guests. Although the problem that the Martins experienced happened several times every week, Juan assumed that the offer of wine and fruit solved the problem.

1. Is the plan for handling incoming guests effective?
2. How important are guest expectations?
3. What might you offer as a solution to prevent this from happening again?
4. What are the potential costs of this incident?

Part Three

STRUCTURE AND POLICIES

*Policies are the epoxy that glue the wheels
of progress*

—UNKNOWN

In a recent speech at the Council on Hotel, Restaurant and Institutional Education (CHRIE) convention, Darryl Hartley-Leonard, president of Hyatt Hotel Corporation, stated that "if a hotel manager who died in 1930 returned to life today, he, and it would be a *he*, could step right in and manage a modern hotel." The message is a strong one. Mr. Hartley-Leonard went on to say that little had changed in the last 60 years in the way of innovative management and that something must be done to prepare the hospitality industry for the twenty-first century.

The hospitality industry has a very strong culture, and many of the traditions have changed little over the last several decades. Managers typically have been trained in the classical management style, with emphasis on planning, organizing, leading, and controlling. Labor has been divided into departments with specific functional responsibilities. At lower levels of the industry, work has been broken into discrete tasks, which enables managers to replace employees with little training necessary. Formal rules and regulations have guided decision making to ensure organizational stability. This type of management system results in strict adherence to rules and regulations; there is often little room for individual freedom, creativity, and innovation. This system demands compliance and often rewards perseverance rather than performance, and those who reach the top of the hierarchy tend to view the world in the same way as their predecessors. This perpetuates a system where things are done the way they have always been done.

Having been presented this rather gloomy picture of the industry you might be thinking: "Can organizations exist without rules, policies, procedures, and structure?" The answer is no, they cannot. These organizational control mechanisms are necessary for the successful operation of all organizations, but it is also necessary to ask occasionally why we do things the way that we do. If the answer is "because we have always done it that way," trouble may be lurking. How does a rule or procedure affect our co-workers and employees? How does it affect guests? A hotel may have a policy of sending a bottle of wine to very unhappy guests without clearly understanding why it has unhappy guests or analyzing the frequency of unhappy guests. Rules and policies are often created for the convenience of managers, but the ultimate test of the utility of the way an organization operates is the value it brings to the guest experience.

Overview of the Incidents

"Rules are made to be broken"—true or false? In the following situations you will see how policies and rules have affected both internal and external customers in organizations in the hospitality industry.

Case 12

The Service Guarantee

Dr. Stinson once had a very unpleasant experience while staying at a nationally known franchise inn. At the time the inn had a corporate service guarantee stating that guests who were not 100 percent satisfied with their accommodations would not have to pay. This particular night the inn was bustling and all the rooms were occupied.

It became apparent that the guests in the room adjoining Dr. Stinson were having a party and were being very loud. Their volume, combined with the thin walls, allowed Dr. Stinson to hear distinctly everything that was being said. She called the front desk about the noise and asked if she could be moved to a different room. The front desk clerk was very abrupt with her, his only response being, "The hotel is sold out tonight, and there is nothing I can do about your problem." In continuing to pursue the problem on the phone, the clerk who was handling Dr. Stinson's complaint was decidedly discourteous, repeating that "the front desk is understaffed, the hotel is very busy tonight, and there is nothing I can do about your problem." After several minutes of somewhat heated discussion, the clerk finally agreed to send someone up to the room next door to request that the occupants of that room bring the noise level down.

Unfortunately, the noise continued unabated. After a considerable amount of time, Dr. Stinson called the front desk a second time. The same front desk clerk with whom she had spoken earlier answered the call and pointed out again that the front office was too busy to take care of her problem. Finally, the people next door left their room.

A few hours later, while the professor was sleeping, the party next door came back. This time not only did their noise disturb her sleep, but their lights did as well as they shone through from under the connecting door. As it was well after midnight, she decided not to complain to the front desk this time, figuring that her only source of satisfaction would be the hotel's guarantee that she would not have to pay for her room.

The next morning, when Dr. Stinson was checking out, she told the front desk clerk that she was not satisfied with her stay and that she didn't want to pay for it. The clerk was not particularly courteous and told Dr. Stinson that she had received no information regarding any guest complaints from the previous night, and the professor would indeed have to pay for her night's stay. Dr. Stinson pointed out to the clerk that the guarantee of the inn stated that a guest who was not satisfied with the stay would not have to pay. At this point the clerk abruptly left her station, saying "I can't do anything about this, you will have to speak to the manager." Several minutes later the manager appeared, and before even discussing the matter simply stated: "Because the hotel was sold out last night, I couldn't have done anything to solve your problem." He refused to honor her request. Dr. Stinson paid for her room but was very upset about the treatment she had received. Following this experience she wrote a letter of complaint to the company, to which she received no response.

1. What impact does a guarantee have on guest expectations?
2. What action might have been taken to resolve the situation?
3. What costs might be associated with this type of situation?

Case 13

The Parking Lot

Jeremy Clegg is the front desk supervisor of the Hotel PennQuid, a distinguished older hotel in Syracuse, New York. Randy Remus is employed by the Hotel PennQuid as the bellstand captain. Joanne Sullivan is a local businesswoman who dines at the hotel's restaurants on a regular basis, often entertaining business clients. She also sends quite a bit of business to the hotel by recommending it to her colleagues and friends. On this particular day, three of her business associates had checked out of their rooms in the hotel following a morning meeting. They were planning on meeting Joanne for lunch at Rugger's, the hotel's casual dining restaurant, after which she would be taking them directly to the airport.

The Hotel PennQuid has a policy that states that only hotel guests and customers of Simon's, the hotel's exclusive restaurant, are provided with valet parking in the hotel lot. Being in an older, downtown location, the hotel's parking is extremely limited. Customers eating at Rugger's are not provided with hotel parking. Although the hotel has 300 rooms, the hotel parking lot has spaces for only 73 cars. After five o'clock, when Simon's does most of its business, it is not a problem for Simon's customers to park their cars in other public lots located nearby. During the day, however, these parking lots lease their spaces by the month to local businesspeople. The hotel has an informal working arrangement with a parking garage located several blocks away to accommodate any overflow. Given its distance, however, the valets prefer not to use it and attempt to ensure that enough spots are available in the hotel lot for a calculated percentage of each day's arriving guests. Over time, they have figured that approximately 30 percent of their guests arrive by car. This percentage goes up on the weekend; however, occupancy goes down, so the number of spaces required remains relatively stable. Often, the only daytime option for Rugger's customers is to park at metered spaces on the street, which are usually difficult to find and may require a walk of several minutes to the hotel.

It was raining when Joanne drove to the hotel for her lunch appointment. As she approached the PennQuid she noticed that the hotel lot was not full and decided she would have her car valet parked. Joanne was somewhat familiar with Jeremy due to her frequent business activities in the hotel, and approached him at the front desk with her request. Jeremy told her that the lot was full, as this was what Randy, the bellstand captain, had told him earlier. She explained to Jeremy that she had just driven by and that there were several vacant spaces in the parking lot. Randy intervened at this time and said that these spots had to be reserved for hotel guests that would be arriving later that afternoon. She then explained that the business associates that she was taking to lunch had been staying at the hotel and that they had just checked out that morning. Randy refused to make an exception for her, and Jeremy reluctantly agreed. Joanne stormed from the hotel and back to her car.

While attempting to find an alternative parking spot, Joanne fumed to herself that the hotel should have definitely made an exception for her, since her associates had been guests in the hotel. Furthermore, she did not accept Randy's policy excuse for not valet parking her car. As she had pointed out to him, there were spaces available in the lot, they would only be eating lunch for an hour at most, and they would be out of the lot before arriving hotel guests would need the space. Walking back to PennQuid in the rain, she remained indignant with the hotel's lack of service and its indifference to regular customers.

Jeremy watched Joanne stride from the hotel and had a boding sense of unease with his decision, but rationalized his action based on the hotel policy and his lack of authority over Randy. Jeremy considered whether he should have fought to make an exception for Joanne, as he knew she was a regular customer who brought business to the hotel. Knowing that he could not order Randy to make such an exception, Jeremy sighed and again felt his frustration with the hotel's chronic problem of not having enough parking for all their guests.

Randy returned to the bellstand shaking his head. Customers seeking parking favors never understood his position or the policy, which was clearly stated on a large sign in the lot: Hotel valet parking is available *only* to registered guests and to customers of Simon's. He felt that if he made an exception for one customer at the front desk, he would soon be asked to make exceptions for everyone. This particular customer's argument that the friends she was meeting for lunch at Rugger's had been guests of the hotel earlier in the day did not sway him. Yes, Randy nodded to himself, he had to be very cautious about keeping spaces available for those legitimately entitled to them. In this way he was keeping the registered guests of the hotel and customers of Simon's happy, as well as minimizing complaints from his staff of parking attendants, who did not have to use the auxiliary parking garage.

1. Evaluate the decision-making process that just took place.
2. Who was right in the interaction?
3. What costs might have been incurred in the situation?

Case 14

The $1 Eggroll

Last week Linda Lowell ordered Chinese food for her family in an attempt to make her life a little less of a hassle. Rather than getting a nice meal quickly and easily, she instead received accusations, abuse, and more stress than she needed.

Linda frequently calls to order food from Ho Cho Ho's Chinese restaurant to be picked up on her way home from work. The last time she had purchased dinner from this establishment, she arrived home to find that the eggroll she had ordered and paid for was not included in the bag. She immediately called the restaurant to report the problem and was told not to worry. The man taking her call explained that the next time she ordered food, she should tell them the situation and they would give her one in its place.

Well, last week, true to her fairly regular pattern, Linda called the restaurant, placed her order, and remembered to mention the missing eggroll, commenting in an understanding voice, "I know how those things can happen, so I'd just appreciate it if you'd put one in free of charge this time."

"Please, what is your phone number, ma'am."

"820–5212," she said, surprised by the question.

"Please hold."

Several minutes later the man returned to the phone and said politely, "I'm sorry, but we have no record of your phone number or your missing eggroll," although his tone implied that Linda would not be receiving one free.

Sighing, Linda replied, "But I wasn't asked my phone number when I called before and reported it, and the gentlemen I spoke with then said it wouldn't be a problem, just to mention it the next time I ordered—which I'm doing," she added more testily.

"Did you get the gentleman's name?"

"No, I didn't even think to ask it because he said it would be no problem."

"Well, I am sorry but I cannot help you because you did not give us your phone number to report your missing eggroll, and that is how we keep a record of such things. We have a very strict policy on this matter as people try to cheat us out of food all of the time. It is quite a problem. If you had gotten the man's name, I might have been able to help you."

Attempting to remain calm, Linda explained, "I can understand your concern about being cheated, but that isn't my problem. My problem is that I wasn't given an eggroll, which I paid for, in my last order, and" her voice rising, "you owe me an eggroll!"

"Please hold," and after a long pause, "No, I am sorry, we cannot give you an eggroll."

Fuming, Linda said, "I have been buying food from your restaurant almost every week for the past two years, and I cannot believe you will not give me the eggroll you owe me."

"Please hold," and then again, "I'm sorry, but you did not give us your phone number, I cannot give you an eggroll."

Linda exploded, "Not only do I no longer want the lousy eggroll you owe me, I don't want the rest of my order either, and not only will I never buy another meal or eggroll from you again, I will tell all of my friends what a terrible experience I've had and that they shouldn't buy your food either!" She was about to slam the phone down when she heard the man say, "Please hold, I will try."

When he returned to the phone for the fourth time, he agreed to give her an eggroll free of charge, but he was quick to scold her, saying "Next time this happens, you make sure you give your phone number and get the name of the person you speak to."

To these directions Linda responded sharply, "Next time, you make sure your employees know what to do," and then banged the phone into its cradle.

Linda went to pick up the food about 10 minutes later. Feeling a little foolish about how angry she had gotten over an eggroll, she chose not to mention the conversation. The man, however, brought it up. He showed her the ticket where it said "One eggroll free," as if to say she was actually getting something free, not something for which she had paid. Heading out the door, she shook her head in amazement and thought, "all of this for a $1 eggroll."

1. What was the cause of this situation?
2. Was either party being unreasonable?
3. What was the potential cost of this interaction?

Case 15

The Minibar Charge

Tim Marler was in a hurry as he left his room at 7:15 A.M. He was checking out of one of New York's finer hotels after a stay of several days. This business trip had been quite successful and he was feeling very good, even though he was running a little late to catch his plane for the West Coast. He had an important meeting early that afternoon in San Francisco, and his schedule was very tight. He chose not to use express or video checkout for two reasons. First, on several occasions in the past, he had incorrect charges on his bill, and reconciling the differences after the fact had been time consuming and irritating. Second, he knew if he turned in his receipts to the accounting department immediately upon return to his office, he was often reimbursed for his expenses before he received his credit card bill and thus avoided covering business expenses with his own money.

As he waited in line at the cashier counter, he kept glancing at his watch—it was now 7:40. Finally arriving at the window, he told the cashier his room number and waited while the computer printed out his bill. The cashier then handed it to him for his perusal. The total was $1063.44. This had been an expensive three-night stay, but he had twice entertained clients at dinner. Upon close examination, Tim noticed that he had been charged $14 for drinks from his minibar, which he had not even opened during his stay. He brought the error to the cashier's attention, to which she responded, "Please wait just a moment, sir, I need to speak to my supervisor about this," and then disappeared into a door behind her. A few minutes later she reappeared with a woman who introduced herself as Madeline, the shift supervisor. She courteously asked Tim, "How can I help you?" It was immediately apparent that the cashier had not explained the situation to her thoroughly, so when Tim said, "There is an error on my bill," the supervisor and cashier began to scrutinize intently the computer printout in front of them.

Several minutes had passed since Tim first stepped up to the counter. The line behind him was growing longer and guests were beginning to grumble. After a brief whispered dialogue between the shift supervisor and the cashier, Madeline said, "I am not authorized to handle this, please wait a moment while I go get the assistant front office manager." Before Tim could say a word, both she and the cashier disappeared into the same door behind the counter. Three or four minutes passed before the assistant manager appeared. She, too, was courteous, but very businesslike. "Are you sure that you did not use the minibar? We seldom make mistakes of this nature." At this point, Tim was aggravated and made it clear that he had not used the minibar. Apparently convinced that Tim was not lying, the assistant manager gave the cashier permission to credit his bill for the $14. While she was doing so, the assistant manager explained that company policy required someone at the assistant manager level or above to authorize changes on discrepancies greater than $10. She then courteously thanked Tim for his business and disappeared through the door. The shift supervisor watched while the cashier made the correction.

At 8:05 A.M. Tim left the cashier's counter with his receipt and raced across the lobby carrying his luggage. He angrily snapped at the doorman to get him a cab and then ordered the cabdriver to get him to the airport as fast as possible. It occurred to him that he might miss his plane and inconvenience an important business client. It was going to be a rotten day.

1. What was the primary cause of this incident?
2. What could have been done to prevent this from happening?
3. What are the costs involved in this situation?

Case 16

100 Percent Occupancy

Kate Wilson lives in New Jersey but commutes to Manhattan two hours each way to work at a prominent New York City hotel as one of four executive-level concierges. She is black, in her early thirties, and has a very positive attitude about life. She typically works the 6 A.M. to 2 P.M. shift. Her warmth and optimism provide a pleasant start to a guest's day.

The U.S. Tennis Open, which occurs for three weeks at the end of August and beginning of September, was taking place. Thousands of players, media, and spectators from around the world had descended on New York to see the games. This hotel, along with most other nearby hotels, was at full capacity, and the general manager required that they have 100 percent occupancy for those three weeks. In this situation the reservations desk overbooked the hotel by a certain percentage and also took walk-ins. Front office personnel had to check in the correct balance of guaranteed reservations and walk-ins to ensure that the hotel was 100 percent full. However, if they did not have enough rooms for guests with guaranteed reservations, they had to "walk" them to another hotel and pay that hotel's rack rate. It was a very stressful situation for front office personnel.

Kate had switched shifts with another concierge, so she was working the late shift on the executive level, from 3 P.M. to 11 P.M. The executive-level floor is popular because it has larger rooms, bigger baths, and an executive floor lounge which serves a continental breakfast, afternoon cookies and tea, and evening cocktails. At the hotel, guests who know they are staying on the executive level can check in either at the front desk, which is in the lobby, or with the executive concierge.

As the evening progressed, Ben, the front office manager, made a decision to sell rooms to walk-ins assuming that guests with guaranteed reservations were not going to arrive. By 10 P.M. the hotel was 100 percent occupied except for two rooms that were being held for guests who might yet arrive with guaranteed reservations. Ben chose not to hold any rooms on the executive-level floor, because "walk-ins" paid the rack rate of $250 for these rooms. This way not only would occupancy be 100 percent but the average room rate would increase. Although he ran the risk of not being able to provide a room on the executive level for a guest with such a guaranteed reservation, Ben felt that the 100 percent occupancy and average room rate increase were more important.

At 10:40 P.M. a guest came to the executive-level floor to check in. After checking in the computer, Kate told the gentleman that the executive level floor was completely occupied but offered him a room on another floor. The gentleman, in a very condescending manner, pulled out his confirmation letter and restated that he had a reservation on that floor. Having stayed on the executive floor before, he was adamant about his reservation. Once again, she told him there were no rooms available on the executive-level floor but that he could have another room. Very angry, he demanded to see the manager. Kate called Ben, who also happened to be the manager on duty that night.

Ben went to the floor quickly and described in more detail the situation at the hotel. He explained the importance of achieving 100 percent occupancy, and given that it was so late at night they did not think he would keep his reservation. Realizing that the guest was still dissatisfied, Ben reiterated that he would get a room on the executive-level floor as soon as one became available. In an attempt to appease this customer, Ben granted him all the executive-level privileges and promised that his first night's stay on the executive level would be complimentary. The man agreed to stay in one of the other regular guest rooms, but made a vow that he would speak to the general manager in the morning. At the end of her shift, Kate went down to the front office to drop off her paperwork and noticed that there were several people at the front desk attempting to register in the fully occupied hotel. She was glad to be going home.

It was not until two days later that the man was placed on the executive-level floor. He did not seem angry at Kate, but he was also not friendly. During his remaining three-day stay on the executive-level floor, he was brisk with her and refused to engage in a relaxed conversation, regardless of Kate's efforts.

1. Is it effective to attempt to achieve 100% occupancy?
2. What are some of the costs incurred in this situation?

Part Four

PROBLEM SOLVING/ DECISION MAKING

One of the tests of leadership is the ability to recognize a problem before it becomes an emergency.
—UNKNOWN

Solving problems and making decisions are two of the most common and important tasks of the hospitality manager. Unfortunately, decisions often begin with problems. Sometimes managers will have adequate time to think about a decision; at other times they will have to respond very quickly. Their experience and level of expertise will often determine if their decision is the correct one.

To be successful at decision making, managers must be able to differentiate problems from symptoms. For example, it is often said that turnover is a problem in the hospitality industry. What do you think—is it? If it is a problem, how do you solve it? Turnover is **not** a problem in the hospitality industry—it is a symptom of a problem. In simple terms, a symptom of a problem is what we see, the problem is the cause of the symptom, and it is the manager's job to diagnose the situation and identify the root cause of a problem. Until this is done, any solution will be a shot in the dark. Once the root cause is identified, we can begin to work toward a solution. Should the manager do this alone? Like many situations in management, it depends.

Decision making has been studied from many perspectives, but one consistent finding from recent research is that the farther decision making can be pushed down the organizational hierarchy, the better, for a number of reasons. First, in this industry, guests and customers do not want to wait for an answer when they have a problem. Decision making can be painfully slow if it has to make its way up and down the hierarchy before action can be taken. Second, those closest to the problem may have the best information to make a decision if they have been well trained. Third, allowing lower-level employees to make decisions sends the message that the manager has faith in their ability. Finally, letting others make decisions gives a manager more of what he or she desperately needs, time to plan for the future.

The place to begin when making a decision is with a simple question: Who will be affected by this decision? If it is an important decision that will affect others significantly, they need to be involved in the decision, or at the very least informed about the decision—how and why it was made as it was.

This involvement will probably improve the quality of the decision and increase the likelihood that others will assist in the implementation of the decision. Time constraints and the magnitude of the problem sometimes make participative decision making impossible or unnecessary, but one of a manager's most important decisions may be who decides.

Overview of the Incidents

People's behavior is rarely random—they decide what to do. It is up to management to assure that both they and their subordinates make the correct decisions. The following situations illustrate what happened to decision making when organizational members lost sight of the overall objective.

Case 17

The Tour Voucher

Kim has worked at the front desk for over a year at a hotel that is located in the Fisherman's Wharf area of San Francisco. Although it is known primarily as a tourist hotel, the property has acquired a reputation for being the best in the area, with approximately 375 rooms, ample meeting space, a gourmet restaurant, and an impeccable service standard.

In the summer months, as tourism increases in the entire city, tour groups frequent the hotel. Group check-ins are done either by the leader, if the group arrives together, or separately if the group is to meet later in the day. On this particular occasion, the group members were checking in separately. It was important that everything run smoothly that day since the entire city was sold out of hotel rooms, due to a major convention.

As the day progressed, more and more people from the tour group checked in. The process was simple: Collect the tour voucher from each person, pull the key packet from the file, where they were sorted by name, take a credit card imprint or cash for incidental charges, and check the person into the computer system. Soon after Mr. Warren and his wife approached the desk ready to check in, Kim's problem began. Even though the Warrens presented Kim with the necessary tour vouchers, they were nowhere in the hotel's records of arriving guests. Kim checked and double-checked the reservations in the computer and checked the listing generated earlier that day by the hotel's reservations manager, Beth. The hotel was already oversold by 30 reservations for that night, as was their policy, so Kim could not remedy the problem immediately simply by accepting the Warrens. After checking several sources of potential information and realizing that the situation would take some time, Kim asked the Warrens if they would like to check their bags with the bellman while she attempted to solve the problem. Reluctantly, they agreed and went to the hotel lobby to wait.

While the Warrens waited patiently, Kim took it upon herself to research the situation, instead of turning the potential guests away. After making phone calls to the tour booking office and checking the corresponding documentation in the sales office, she still could not discover the reason for the problem. When she went into the reservations office, she checked with Beth, one of the reservationists, to see if the information could be pulled up on their computers. Unfortunately, no additional information was found, but luckily, Beth kept strict records of the tour group bookings in the files. Kim discovered that the reservation had been faxed through to the hotel as an addition to the original tour group listing, but for some reason, the reservation had never been made in the computer. Having determined that it was the hotel's problem and not that of the tour booking office, Kim took it upon herself to check the Warrens in. Her reasoning was that, after all, the hotel would be turning away guests later that day anyway. Although the Warrens were clearly annoyed at the situation, they were understanding and extremely relieved when the problem was finally remedied.

Unfortunately, Kim's extra efforts were seemingly unappreciated. She had managed to keep the situation relatively quiet while other tour group members were checking in, thus reducing the amount of embarrassment to the hotel and its staff. Beth ignored the fact that it was her mistake and let Kim handle the entire situation. The sales manager who handled the tour group bookings was annoyed that Kim had been calling to find out more information on the situation. Little support was given by the other members of the staff as well, with the exception of Hope, the front office manager, who understood that her staff was under an extreme amount of stress due to the hotel's projected occupancy for that evening. This was not the first time an incident such as this had occurred at this hotel. It seems, however, that the hotel has adopted the position that the system had worked basically in the past—why change it?

1. Evaluate Kim's response to the situation.
2. What do you think of the overbooking policy?
3. What improvements might you suggest for the system?

Case 18

The Headwaiter

Per is a 25-year-old headwaiter who is responsible for banquets and the restaurant of a medium-sized hotel in Brussels, Belgium. The hotel is one of many old, traditional, family owned and operated hotels in Brussels. Per was educated at the Hotel School in Lausanne, Switzerland, is dedicated to his profession, and is determined to do a good job serving guests of the hotel. Unfortunately, Per is often faced with frustrating situations, such as the following description of a single day.

It is Saturday afternoon and there is a wedding reception at the hotel. In the lounge 100 people are drinking champagne and waiting for the bride and the bridegroom. The hotel has everything ready for a wonderful evening for the guests. The host of the wedding receives a telephone call from the best man, explaining that the bride and bridegroom are delayed at the photographer's. That seems to be no problem for the host, and he contacts Per to tell him the news. Then he asks Per for more champagne for everyone so they do not have empty glasses when the bride and bridegroom arrive. Unbeknownst to the host, Per has only a limited number of bottles of that brand of champagne, which the store clerk delivered to him earlier that day. Per had ordered enough for only one to one and a half glasses of champagne per guest, due to the projected arrival time of the wedding party. Even though there is more champagne in the beverage storeroom, none of the wait staff can get in, as only the store clerk and the general manager have keys. The store clerk seldom works on weekends, so Per first tries to call the general manager and owner of the hotel, to have him drive to the hotel and get more champagne out of the storeroom. The general manager lives less than 10 minutes by car from the hotel, and this is his plan for dealing with this type of situation. The general manager is not at home, however, so Per goes to the restaurant and the bar of the hotel and collects all the bottles of champagne and sparkling wine they can give him. He then approaches the host of the wedding to explain that they have to change to different labels for the extra serving. The host says he thinks it is strange that they cannot get more champagne out of the storeroom, and he really wants the brand of champagne the groom had ordered. Per can do nothing and the guest is very unhappy.

Early that same evening a party of 14 businesspeople who had reserved a table arrive at the hotel restaurant. They have arranged for a fixed meal, but they want to order wine when they arrive, after discussing the selection with the headwaiter. The host wants to request the most expensive wine for his party. Unfortunately, the restaurant has only four bottles of that wine available, as the rest are in the storeroom. Per has to recommend a less expensive wine so that he has enough bottles for the entire party, to which the host reluctantly agrees.

It is now late evening in the bar of the hotel. Four people are drinking their favorite brand of cognac. After two rounds of drinks they ask for another serving of cognac, but the bartender has only two drinks left in the bottle. Since it is a seldom-called-for brand of cognac, the bartender has only this bottle. Therefore he calls the headwaiter, and asks for another bottle. Per cannot help, because he has no keys to the storeroom. All he can do is to go to the table and explain to the guests that the hotel is sold out of that brand, and recommend another brand. Although the guests are not overly concerned and they order another brand, for Per it is one more bitter reminder that he cannot always give guests what they want.

Per tried several strategies to prevent these incidents from happening. First, he tried to change the system so that he or someone else had keys to the storeroom in the evenings, since almost all wine sales occurred in the evenings. The general manager refused to discuss this issue at all and would not give a key to anyone. When this strategy did not work, Per started calling the manager each time they needed anything from the storeroom. By doing this he hoped that the manager would get tired of being called and realize that he had to do something about this situation. The manager usually came down and took out of the storeroom whatever the headwaiter (or ultimately the guests) wanted and then went back home. The general manager did not seem to be bothered that he was called quite often or that the hotel guests experienced a delay in their service.

Per then tried another strategy: ordering more beverages than he needed from the storeroom when there was a banquet or a party to ensure that he would have enough. After Per returned several unopened bottles following a large party the store clerk began to anticipate this and he gave Per fewer beverages than he ordered. When Per tried to talk to the manager about the problem, the manager said that the employees of the hotel should learn to say no to the guests more often. Per's final strategy was to set up an auxiliary storeroom, to which he had access. This seemed like a good idea, but he was allowed to store only a few bottles of several of the best-selling brands. This did not help the situation, as it was demand for unusual, expensive brands that typically created a problem.

Per has become very tired of fighting the management and the store clerk to satisfy the customers. In the beginning he was committed to giving the customers what they wanted. Currently, Per has resigned himself to giving less than excellent service, often telling guests that what they want is locked in the storeroom and it cannot be taken out. Although it discourages Per further that the guests do not perceive him as being helpful, he rationalizes that management obviously does not want him to be helpful toward the guests.

1. Who do you think is right in this situation?
2. Why do you think the general manager has this policy?
3. What messages are being sent by the general manager?
4. What do you think Per might do in the future?

Case 19

It Stinks

Brad Howard is an organizational consultant who travels quite frequently. On this occasion he arrived at the airport and went directly to the auto rental agency to pick up his car. Behind the counter stood a young lady in her rental company uniform and two young men in overalls. The reservation had been made for the wrong-size car, but the travel agent, not the rental agency, was at fault. As Brad walked away from the desk with the keys to the car he wondered if he was getting the best rate.

After walking about 300 yards to where the rental cars were parked, Brad found his car. In his words, "I got in the car and there was this overwhelming air freshener smell, just unbelievable, and it practically made me gag. It smelled very bad, it wasn't even pleasant air freshener. I thought it would be too much of a hassle to change cars and I didn't want to have to rehandle huge bag that I had packed for a week of travel. Instead, I opened the windows, turned on the car, opened the vents, and turned the ventilation system on high. They must also have sprayed the vents because all of a sudden this odor, like toxic gas, came at me and instantly permeated my clothes. I drove around the parking lot once and decided it was not getting any better. So I parked the car and lugged my bag back to the terminal. By this time I was very angry."

Upon arrival back at the rental counter, the attendant simply said, "You're back." Brad told her what had happened and she did not respond but instead acted as if Brad had inconvenienced her. When he told her his clothes smelled, a customer nearby said, "I can smell it." This customer then turned to the attendant and said, "I told you about that the last time I was here. You really need to change your air freshener." The attendant gave Brad a different car, but offered no upgrade, no assistance, no discount, and gave no indication that the rental company had done anything wrong. As Brad was about to leave the counter, she said, "Oh, sorry about that." He again carried his luggage back to the parking lot and found his car. It was indeed better and he drove off to begin his business. He began to think of how much this was going to cost the rental agency.

His thinking ran this way, "Using old math to figure out if you made a profit or a loss you would begin with the rental of about $150 for three days. I figure their operating margin is somewhere around 10 percent so their operating profit is $15. I am continuing to rent the car, so using old math, this is a $15 win for them. With new math, I look at it this way. The dry cleaning is going to cost them about $12. I am going to have to write them a letter to get them to pay this, so its going to cost them about $15 to process the complaint. The average check processing fee is $8 just to cut a check, and they are going to have to re-prep the car, which is about $10, so the total is about $45. Now if you go back to the other model, their operating profit was $15, so they actually had a loss of $30 on this transaction."

Brad continued, "In terms of my cost, the time to replace the car and going through this hassle cost me about 30 minutes plus 15 minutes to write a letter. I bill out at $188.50 an hour, so that's $140 plus $1 for the paper and stamp, for a total of $141. Take that together with the $150 rental, and the overall cost of the rental has effectively doubled for me. Now what kind of company can survive in the marketplace when they double the cost of a rental?"

Brad turned serious and wanted to talk about the bigger implications of this situation. "On average, I rent a car two days a week and my company is paying about $50 per day for a rental. That's $100 per rental, 50 weeks per year, for a total of $5000. There are ten people in my office who travel as much or more than I do. That's over $50,000 per year that we are spending. We are now deciding whether or not to stay with our current rental company, and I thought I would give this company a try as I had always believed that they were a quality organization. I am a member of the management committee of my firm and, based on this experience, I will be arguing strongly to stay with our present company."

When asked if there was any way the company could have recovered from the situation, Brad said that there was—"if they would have offered an upgrade or a reduced rate, or, more important, gone all out to help me. Even something like having someone go pick up the car or offering to pay for my dry cleaning might have satisfied me. I don't know if it would have made a difference for sure because it did not happen, but I suspect I would at least have given them another chance."

1. Why did this situation come about?
2. What were the service recovery opportunities?
3. What are the potential costs of this transaction?

Case 20

The Portland Hotel

The Portland Hotel is a 500-room business hotel in Portland, Oregon. Its mission statement commits the hotel to provide the best lodging possible by empowering its employees, known as associates, and providing them with incentives to create extraordinary customer service and shareholder value. The associates are recognized as internal customers, and the needs of these customers include having the resources, skills, and the motivation to perform their job. The Portland Hotel makes every effort to meet these needs with appropriate expenditures, employee training, and an overall company culture that inspires associates to perform at their peak.

Concierge personnel at the Portland Hotel are not only responsible for the traditional functions of a downtown hotel concierge but also handle the operations of the executive floor, located at the top of the hotel. This includes such tasks as the preparation, setup, and presentation of two meals every day that are available in the executive floor lobby, monitoring the stock at the honor bar, and responding to special requests of the VIPs who typically stay on this level. Kimberly Martin, one of the five concierges employed at the hotel, is responsible for covering all of these tasks at any given time and, with the use of a property management computer system terminal on the executive floor, she is capable of doing so. The computer on the executive floor was critical to the success of the concierge's job for two reasons. First, the concierge can answer any type of front-office-related questions because of the automated access to occupancy, room status, guest history, and folio information from the computer. Second, at the end of each evening the concierge can directly input all beverage revenues from the honor bar onto the appropriate folio without leaving the floor. In both cases Kimberly can remain on the floor and always be available to provide personal attention, which is part of delivering the best possible customer service to this floor's clientele.

Although both occupancy and profitability had increased over the past year, the management of the hotel felt it necessary to attempt to save money where possible. They decided to reduce costs by decreasing the number of computer terminals in the hotel, including the one located on the executive floor. According to management, the benefits involved with having a computer on the executive floor did not outweigh the costs.

Kimberly's reaction to the removal of the computer was one of frustration, as she had to leave the floor unattended for several times during a shift and could not always be available to assist guests when needed. She was also angry that none of the concierges were notified about the decision prior to having the terminal removed, nor had they been given any explanation as to how this cost-cutting measure might benefit the overall hotel. Furthermore, they had not been given an opportunity to explain what a crucial role it played in the performance of their job. Kimberly felt betrayed by the hotel in that she no longer had the resources she needed to ensure guest satisfaction. Often when she returned to the floor after the now necessary absences, she was confronted by guests who had grown impatient waiting for service. The frequency of these encounters prompted her to ask that another terminal be placed on the executive floor but her request was denied. Her inability to provide guests with the best possible service, and her perception that management was not responding to the needs of the front line employees, led to Kimberly's loss of motivation and commitment to the organization.

1. Was the decision to remove the terminal necessary? For whom?
2. What present and future costs are involved in this decision?

Case 21

The Ski Trip

Amanda Boyer, a special accounts claims manager for a large commercial insurance company, and her husband Chad had decided to spend a long holiday weekend skiing in Killington, Vermont. Amanda realized that Killington would be a popular destination because of the holiday and made reservations early with a hotel in the area. Neither Amanda nor Chad, a full-time graduate student, had the time or inclination to research information about smaller independent inns in Killington. Instead, they readily settled on a Quality Lodge, a national chain that had recently opened a motel in the area. They had both stayed in other Quality Lodges and had been satisfied with the service and accommodations. They were pleased to secure a reservation with the one in Killington, feeling safe in their expectations of what it would be like. They drove from Cincinnati on a Friday afternoon anticipating a memorable weekend.

The 12-hour drive, the last bit in heavy snow, left the couple exhausted and ready for a good night's sleep. They arrived close to midnight at the Quality Lodge. The property was constructed on a large plot of land and consisted of several two-story buildings, each of which contained a number of rooms. The front desk registration area was located in a separate building apart from any of the guestrooms. Upon arrival, the two checked in and chatted with the front desk clerk about the weekend conditions. They learned that, unfortunately, temperatures were dropping and, with wind-chill, would reach between 30 and 60 degrees below zero. The clerk assured them both, however, that the new hotel was well insulated and that the heating system was more than adequate. Amanda and Chad drove to the building containing their suite with visions of a warm, comfortable room. They instead entered an icy-cold sitting room and an even colder bedroom. The heating unit had not been running and the thermostat registered 40°F. They turned the heater and fan on "high," and after listening to it clang for 5 minutes and detecting only a trace of heat, they called the front desk to report the problem. The same clerk with whom they had spoken earlier apologized for the inconvenience and said that she would move them. Amanda suspected that the hotel was full and questioned the clerk, who assured them that by the time they drove back to the front desk she would be able to assign them another room. When they tramped from their car back into the registration office, she again apologized and said, "I made a mistake. We are all booked for the weekend so you will have to stay in your current room." She continued more brightly, "However, here is a space heater you can use. It should heat up your room in no time." The front desk agent pointed to a cumbersome 40-pound electric heater. By this time it was quarter to one in the morning and Amanda knew that if they were going to get any sleep, or heat, that night they had no choice but to take the heater without further delay or discussion. Together they squeezed it into the still-packed car and carried it to the room.

Although they did not express their extreme displeasure with the front desk clerk, they were shocked and furious about how they had been treated. Indignant that they had been tricked in to returning to the registration office to collect the space heater, they felt the least the clerk should have done to resolve the problem was have a hotel employee deliver it. They concluded that the Quality Lodge did not care about their guests, as the clerk was more concerned about not rousing someone on the maintenance staff than she was with providing service. Even with the space heater plugged in, the only thing really hot in the room was Amanda and her husband. Off to a bad start at the hotel, their unresolved anger affected the rest of their stay, causing them to view the slightest imperfections in the hotel as major defects, which they generalized to the rest of the chain.

1. Was anyone really at fault in this situation?
2. Why do you think the heater was not turned on in the room?
3. Who is hurt by the Boyers' experience and conclusions?

Part Five

COMMUNICATION

Information is the lifeblood of organizations.
—MARGARET WHEATLEY[1]

Organizations are systems. If you will for a moment think of the human body as a system, there are close parallels that you can use to better understand how systems operate. Within the human system we have vital organs that we depend on for normal functioning. The brain, kidneys, liver, heart, and lungs all have specific functions but are dependent on each other to sustain life. The coordination mechanism is the nervous system, and the circulatory system provides fuel for the various organs. Hospitality organizations are typically composed of functional areas such as accounting, marketing and sales, food and beverage, housekeeping, front office, and engineering. The flow of communication provides the coordination and information necessary for this type of organization to function properly. Organization structure, focus on functional specialization, conflicting objectives, or differing hierarchical level can all create communication barriers. Similar to the human body, if this flow is interrupted or inefficient, the organization will suffer.

Managers often think that their subordinates do not need to be informed about issues and decisions. Occasionally, this is true, but it is important to understand what happens when information is lacking. A recent study of a European hotel company going through difficult times revealed that the quantity of information shared with employees during this time decreased dramatically. This was accompanied by plummeting job satisfaction and increased turnover, and declines in guest satisfaction. Instead of keeping employees informed during this troubled time, management believed it was best to keep the information to themselves. Employees need to know what is expected of them, why things are being done as they are, and they must receive feedback on their performance.

Managers must also recognize that the informal communication network, the grapevine, is extremely efficient at distributing information quickly throughout an organization. Tapping into the grapevine can provide a manager with timely information, but without accurate information the grapevine will quickly be spreading inaccurate information in the form of rumors.

Customers and guests are also part of this system and they have needs for information as well. If there is a breakdown in the communication process their expectations may not be met. Furthermore, involving guests or customers by communicating honestly and appropriately with them may be what is necessary to resolve their dissatisfaction or anger. Communication is the first step toward service recovery.

Overview of the Incidents

In the hospitality industry many errors occur repeatedly because of poor communication. In times of stress, the desire or need for information may increase. The following situations illustrate the effect that communication processes and systems have had on both internal and external customers.

Endnote

[1]Margaret Wheatley, *Leadership and the New Science*. San Francisco: Berrett-Koehler, 1992.

Case 22

The Shared Suite

Mark Williams is a professional in the hospitality industry who has worked at the operations level in several hotels and clubs and has extensive experience as a human resources consultant. His ongoing industry involvement prompted him to participate in a hospitality industry conference held in Nashville, Tennessee. Mr. Williams' stay at the hotel during the convention was characterized by frustration, confusion, and poor guest service.

The incident that spoiled his visit at the hotel occurred within the first few hours of his arrival in the early evening. Mr. Williams had confirmed reservations at the hotel held under two names, his own and Michael Thompson. Mr. Williams' plan was to share a two-bedroom suite with Mr. Thompson so that they could have a space to work together during free hours. Mr. Williams was the first of the pair to arrive at the hotel. He checked in at the front desk, received his room assignment, and told the reservations agent that Mr. Thompson would be checking in within the next few hours. Mr. Williams then had his luggage sent up to his room and went to an educational seminar on the other side of the hotel. Minutes later, the other gentleman checked in at the front desk and found his way to the suite he was to be sharing with Mr. Williams. Upon entry, he decided that he was not satisfied with the bedroom that he had been given, as it had a sleep sofa instead of an actual bed. He immediately called the front desk to arrange for a room change. He left a note for Mr. Williams explaining that he was moving them to a different suite and that the front desk would have the new room number. The front desk immediately sent a bellman who escorted Mr. Thompson to a larger suite that satisfied his needs. After settling into his new room, Mr. Thompson went to the lobby bar to meet a colleague.

One hour later, Mr. Williams returned to his original room, found the note from Mr. Thompson, and called the front desk to get the new room number. As Mr. Williams was not registered in the new room the front desk clerk would not give out the number, but instead connected him to the new room. He received a busy signal. Over the course of the next hour, Mr. Williams continued to attempt to call Mr. Thompson, yet the line remained busy. Eventually, Mr. Williams felt that the room that he was calling might be the room that he was currently in, so he called the front desk to straighten out the misunderstanding. The front desk clerk told him that the room he was in was classified as unoccupied, and that she could not give him the other gentlemen's new number because the computer was down. She then instructed Mr. Williams to remain in his room until the computer came back on-line and then she would call him to straighten out the situation. While waiting in his room for the return phone call, a stranger opened Mr. William's door and walked into the room. Each person was shocked by the encounter, and the stranger's shock quickly turned into anger. A confrontation erupted and Mr. Williams was forced to calm the stranger and explain the complicated situation. After convincing the stranger that a simple mistake had been made due to computer problems, Mr. Williams called the front desk to report that someone had been assigned to this room, and a bellman was immediately sent to move the stranger to a different room.

One hour later, Mr. Williams received a call from the front desk informing him of Mr. Thompson's room number. As it was very late, Mr. Williams had prepared for bed and told the clerk that he was planning to sleep in his original room, however, he felt that he should not be billed for the one night's stay due to the hotel's mishandling of his transfer to the other suite. The clerk initially resisted his request and then agreed that the cost of the room would be credited to his account in the morning. The next morning, Mr. Williams moved his luggage to the other room and went to the front desk to confirm that his bill for one night's stay had been credited. The clerk at the front desk informed Mr. Williams that she had no record of a credit on his bill and directed him to speak with the manager on duty. Mr. Williams explained the entire situation to the manager on duty, who was both skeptical about the content of the story and reluctant to credit the bill. After 20 minutes of conversation, the manager agreed to credit Mr. Williams' account. Only at this point could Mr. Williams put the incident behind him and with peace of mind begin to focus his attention on attending the conference.

1. What was the primary cause of this situation?
2. How was it further complicated? Why?
3. What could have been done to prevent the occurrence of any of this?

Case 23

The Flight from Norway

Lillian Sorensen had arrived on her flight from Norway to Newark, New Jersey, at 12:45 P.M. on a cold, gray day in mid-March. She had planned to go on from there to Ithaca, New York, with a domestic airline that was affiliated with the international carrier. Her scheduled departure time from Newark was 4:30 P.M., and her scheduled arrival time in Ithaca was approximately 6:00 P.M.

When she checked in at the domestic airline they told her to be back a half an hour before departure because there was a bus that would drive her from the terminal to the airplane. She waited near the ticket counter, and at 4:30 P.M. she was worried that she had missed the bus to the plane. Ten minutes later the public address system informed her that the flight to Ithaca was delayed. There was no explanation given, and one and a half hours later the passengers were called to board the plane.

It was a small, older plane and its deteriorated appearance prompted several passengers to comment on its lack of maintenance and question its safety in the air. The flight attendant brushed aside these concerned inquiries from the passengers, claiming defensively that it was not her fault they were late or that it was an older plane, summed up in her comment, "This is not my usual route." After the engines on the plane had started and the passengers had received the standard security presentation, the captain came on the intercom to say that they were experiencing "technical difficulties" but the passengers should remain seated because they should be able to remedy the situation quickly. The captain then came back into the passenger cabin to retrieve a manual from the rear of the plane, then returned to the cockpit.

It was very cold in the plane because no heat was on and it became even colder when two mechanics came into the passenger cabin, leaving the exterior door open. The mechanics proceeded to remove several plates from the ceiling of the passenger cabin and began to work. There was no explanation given to the passengers, who were watching the mechanics make repairs. After approximately 30 minutes, the passengers were removed from the plane and taken back to the terminal.

Upon arrival at the terminal the passengers received no explanation from the ground employees, who apparently did not know anything about the extent of the repairs being made or of the passengers' continued delay. At 7:00 P.M. they were informed that the flight had been canceled and the airline offered to provide a bus to Ithaca directly from Newark. The passengers had no desire to take a six-hour bus ride, so the airline said they would attempt to arrange alternative flight arrangements to Ithaca. At 7:15 P.M. the passengers all received a meal voucher for $10.00 along with a message to be back at 7:30 as there was a chance that they could depart on the next flight going toward Ithaca. When Lillian returned back after 15 minutes and a hasty meal, she was informed that the passengers could not be taken to Ithaca with the next plane, but that they would be flown to Elmira, a city 50 miles from Ithaca, and then be transported the remainder of the distance by bus.

The flight was scheduled to depart at 8:00 P.M., but at that time it was announced that the flight would be delayed and the boarding time would now be 9:30 P.M. Lillian explained to the individual at the ticket counter that she had been traveling for the last 20 hours and it was the middle of the night on her time. She asked if there was some place to sit where someone could let her know when the plane was ready because she was afraid she would go to sleep and the plane would leave without her. No attempt was made to accommodate her regarding this request, nor were the airline employees helpful in directing her when she asked to make a phone call so that she could notify her friends who would be picking her up at the Ithaca airport. In response to the airline staff's indifference and her extreme exhaustion, resignation to accept the situation was Lillian's only alternative.

Lillian did finally board a plane at 9:30 P.M., but upon arrival in Elmira at 11:30 P.M., found the airline office closed and no waiting bus. The pilots and the flight attendant quickly left the airport, again offering no explanation or encouragement. Some of the passengers rented a car and drove themselves to Ithaca. The remaining passengers, including Lillian, waited approximately 40 minutes before three vans arrived to take them to Ithaca. The van that Lillian entered first delivered people, who had been already seated, to various locations in Elmira, then started the drive to Ithaca. With an additional delay due to the bus driver getting lost, Lillian arrived at the Ithaca airport at 2:00 A.M., eight hours later than expected.

1. How might this situation have been handled differently?
2. Why do you think it happened as it did?
3. What is the airline's interest in withholding information?

Case 24

Room Service, Please

Steven, an emigrant from Peru, is a room service waiter at a AAA Five Diamond luxury hotel in Washington, D.C. Guests in this hotel desire excellent service in elegant surroundings, not only the "best" service on a scale relative to other hotels, but "flawless" service on an absolute scale. Steven has been in his position for nearly 10 years, the second-longest tenure in the room service department. He is highly skilled in his profession, works hard, and has both an excellent command of the English language and superior attention to detail.

Within the room service department there is a distinct division of duties. The room service cashier receives guest orders, either by phone or via doorknob cards collected by the night staff. The orders are written down by the room service cashier and then passed on to both the kitchen staff and the waiters. Cashiers receive virtually no training and little on-the-job coaching or support. There is only one cashier assigned per shift, regardless of variability in demand, and therefore the cashier is frequently overburdened at peak times. The cashier's only official duties are to take telephone orders and operate the point-of-sale system. During slack times when the cashier has nothing to do, managers frequently assign him or her to other duties within the department. If a rush occurs when the cashier is away from the station, the phone may go unanswered and room service orders can easily fall behind.

Room service waiters assemble the carts and pick up the meals from the kitchen, deliver the meals to the guest room, and return the signed guest receipt to the cashier. Until the waiter arrives at the guest's door with the ready meal, he or she has not communicated with the guest regarding the order. Few of the waiters are cross-trained in the cashier's duties, so they are unable to assist in the cashier function.

This renowned Washington hotel has a recurring problem with incorrect room service orders or orders being delivered to the wrong room. The majority of such incidents involve missing items or items cooked differently than the guest requested. In this particular incident, Steven delivered breakfast to a guest at 6:30 A.M. After knocking gently on the door and quietly announcing "room service," Steven waited several minutes then announced his arrival again, somewhat louder this time. He heard noise in the room and an angry voice shouted "Just a minute!" The door then flew open and a tall middle-aged man in his bathrobe began to scream at Steven that he had not ordered room service and was greatly disturbed by being awakened at this early hour. The order pad had listed the wrong room! The guest then slammed the door and called the front desk to complain. It then took Steven and the cashier about 15 minutes to figure out the room number of the guest who had actually ordered breakfast. The breakfast order, now a bit old, was rushed to the correct guest, who scolded Steven for being late. Steven apologized and informed the guest that there would be no charge for breakfast.

When Steven returned to the room service office, he started an altercation with the cashier. "How could you get the room number wrong?" The remaining waiters joined in, and a major fracas occurred during peak serving hours. The manager reprimanded the cashier severely in front of the wait staff. Later that day, the front office manager provided a free lunch to the erroneously awakened guest and his wife. Despite encouraging words from his manager, Steven went home feeling discouraged and frustrated. One small mistake resulted in two annoyed guests, three free meals, and increased employee tension. Management did nothing to prevent the problem from occurring again.

1. What is the cause of this situation?
2. What are the costs involved in this situation?
3. What recommendations might you have to improve the system?

Case 25

Rob Jones Corporation

Over a period of three years, Laura Hollings rose through the ranks of the front desk area and sales division of the distinguished Cameron Hotel to attain the position of sales manager. She had worked very hard to achieve this position and had demonstrated an ability to deal effectively with clients and secure new accounts. She had been working as a sales manager for approximately a year when the sales manager in charge of the Rob Jones' account was promoted and transferred to another of the chain's hotels. Laura took over the account.

The Rob Jones Corporation is basically a motivational and instructional institute that holds seminars at the Cameron Hotel. Rob Jones started the corporation many years ago and it is a very important client for the hotel, accounting for approximately $500,000 per year in rooms, restaurant, and meeting space revenues. The self-development seminars focus on improving managerial and interpersonal skills and time management. The usual size of these seminars is over 100 people and all of the staff know when this account is "in house." The clients of Rob Jones are managers from various corporations located in the southwestern United States. These guests are considered very important to the hotel not only during the seminar but after, as they represent possible future hotel revenues when they are traveling for their own business or pleasure. Rob Jones himself is extremely meticulous and expects those people with whom he conducts business to be like-minded, with a focus on every detail of the stay or of a request. The level of service is expected to be exceptional, and special effort is placed on these meetings to ensure a smooth stay for everyone associated with Rob Jones.

The situation that was now bothering Mr. Jones was cumulative, having built over the period of several of months. He first noticed that errors were being made with some of the specifications of his meeting rooms and with the food items that he had requested. Initially, he did not protest since the service of the hotel had been so good in the past, and he viewed the problems as abnormalities that did not demand his involvement. However, the errors did not stop and grew from a minor irritation to a serious issue for Mr. Jones. He was not satisfied with the service that was being provided and blamed the hotel. Laura was the contact for Mr. Jones and she talked to him about some of the problems that he was having. He mentioned that room listings were often incorrect and that conference room requests that he made had not been fulfilled. Laura promised to correct these problems and assured him that they would not happen again. Unfortunately, Laura was negligent with her follow-up and the problems continued with the same frequency.

Angered by the lack of attention being given to his seminars, Mr. Jones canceled his next meeting with the hotel. A shock alarm went throughout the Cameron, as all departments of the hotel would be affected. The director of sales became involved at this point and gathered an assortment of managers to work through the problem. Representatives from every department were assembled and they all went bearing cookies and apologies to the office of Mr. Jones on a sales call to try to win back his business. He was impressed with this new attitude and happily accepted the apology and rescheduled his seminar.

As part of the agreement to return to the hotel, Mr. Jones wanted a guarantee that the recent problems would not happen again. Laura scheduled a meeting between herself and Mr. Jones to address any specific concerns that Mr. Jones might still have. Laura had to miss that meeting, but she did inform Mr. Jones beforehand and rescheduled for a later date, promising at the time that she was interested in hearing his feedback. The rescheduled meeting never took place. Laura had taken the day off the day it was rescheduled and missed the meeting completely, not bothering to call Mr. Jones or inform anyone else of the meeting. That was the final straw for Mr. Jones. He vowed never to return and cancelled all future meetings with the hotel.

The general manager, who had previously been monitoring the situation through the director of sales, now took over. He had relied on the director of sales to ensure that the situation was under control. With the cancellation of the future seminars, he fired Laura on the spot, reprimanded the director of sales, and then prepared himself for a "grovel call." He personally went to apologize to Mr. Jones and beg him for his business. The general manager, Bruce Adams, informed Mr. Jones of Laura's immediate termination and committed himself to be personally responsible for all future contact if Mr. Jones would agree to return. Bruce exhorted the hotel's philosophy of intolerance to service deficiencies, reiterated his desire to exceed customer expectations, stated how important Mr. Jones was to him, and offered major concessions in terms of discounts on room rates and dining. Finally, Bruce begged Mr. Jones for the opportunity to make up for the past mistakes and to hold him personally responsible if things went wrong. Bruce was persuasive and Mr. Jones did relent and return his business to the hotel. The general manager is still handling the Rob Jones account and will be for some time, until Mr. Jones's respect and confidence are renewed.

1. What went wrong in this situation? Why?
2. How could it have been prevented?
3. What are some of the costs associated with the situation?

Case 26

The Wounded Bird

Chris, a professor of sociology, and his wife were returning home from vacation in San Diego. Chris is a particularly cautious man and, as a father of four, felt that they should travel separately so that in the event of a fatal accident, the children would not be orphaned. They both flew on a major airline and did in fact take different flights, Chris's trip being on an L1011 wide-body plane to Chicago. As they approached the airport, the plane began to descend at a rate that seemed very fast to Chris. The plane began to bounce violently as it approached the runway. The only way for the pilot to regain control was to accelerate the engine and redirect the plane back up into the air. The passengers immediately asked the flight attendants what was happening, and they were told that the plane was unable to land in Chicago due to wind ground speed in excess of 70 miles per hour at O'Hare Airport. Once back at cruising altitude, the passengers were informed that they were being rerouted to Nashville, where weather conditions were good. During the aborted landing in Chicago, several passengers and one flight attendant fainted. Passengers were offered complimentary beverage service during the rerouted flight to Nashville, though few accepted. Chris noted that only two of the flight attendants were particularly good at calming the passengers and answering their questions throughout the ordeal.

They landed in Nashville around 11:30 P.M. with no apparent problems. However, Chris found it odd that emergency vehicles were on the runway to meet the plane. After entering the terminal and checking a monitor he realized that other scheduled planes had been delayed, and kept circling in the air, until the L1011 was on the ground. He also overheard one of the Nashville airport employees say, "Here come the people from that wounded bird." Although the airline personnel revealed only that a small repair had become necessary, Chris learned that the real reason they were unable to land in Chicago was because one of the wing flaps was inoperable. The realization of the danger of their earlier situation left him shaken.

After some confusion in the terminal, the passengers were eventually told that their flight would reboard for Chicago in an hour. Chris immediately went to a airline desk to try to figure out a way to contact his wife, who he believed would be waiting for him at O'Hare. He was told that they could try to have her paged but the information regarding his flight would be readily available in Chicago so she would not be worried. He accepted that, but then went to a pay phone to try to contact the babysitter at his home to explain the situation. He found that his wife had also called and that she was indeed waiting for him at O'Hare. He returned to the airline desk and insisted that they page her. Fifteen minutes later he was able to speak with her, and she said that she would wait for him to arrive, as she did not want to make the one hour drive home alone at that time of night. Quite some time later it was announced that their original plane was not immediately repairable because of a missing part, and therefore a substitute plane had been located to take them to Chicago. However, this plane also needed repairs before it would be ready for flight. Although it was now almost 1:00 A.M., the passengers were not offered additional complimentary beverages or food while waiting in Nashville, nor were there any offers of hotel accommodations for those who chose to stay over. Several passengers made alternative flight arrangements to reach their final destinations. Chris waited in the terminal another four hours and eventually returned to Chicago that morning at approximately 7:00 A.M. His wife was waiting for him as he entered the lobby. She was very happy to see him, but exhausted and extremely angry with the airline.

1. Is it appropriate to lie to a customer?
2. Compare the airline's interest in withholding information to passengers' interest in having it.
3. What could have been done to improve the situation?

Case 27

The Three-Hour Brunch

Matt Robinson and five of his friends decided to have Sunday brunch at a suburban restaurant. Upon arrival, the six customers were seated quickly at the back of the restaurant and the host was prompt in giving them menus. It took them a few minutes to decide what each would be having, after which they closed their menus. They sat talking casually for the next 10 minutes, thinking that their waitress would be coming shortly. As their wait stretched into 20 minutes, they became noticeably impatient, checking their watches and attempting to make eye contact with someone on the wait staff. Finally, after 30 minutes, an angry Matt left the table to find a someone to wait on them. Cindy, the waitress he spoke with, informed them that she was not assigned to their section but would take their order anyway. It seemed to Matt that Cindy was quite nervous. Although she had served every table around them, she did not seem to want to wait on a large party of young men.

Everyone at the table ordered their meal and Cindy left to get their drinks and find out who was supposed to be serving their table. She quickly returned just to tell them that she would, in fact, be their waitress. She then headed back into the kitchen, presumably to get their drinks, but returned again empty-handed except for the tab for the table. Another 30 minutes had passed when Matt flagged down a different waitress, who agreed to check on their food. When this waitress returned, she had the drinks they had ordered so long ago. Much to their surprise, however, she did not serve them, but instead placed all of the drinks on the table behind them for Cindy to distribute. As Cindy was nowhere to be seen, the party decided to serve themselves. Cindy finally appeared with a large tray of food for the table, but it was not what any of them had ordered. When they told her this she proceeded to the table next to them and asked the people there if they had ordered any of the food that she was carrying. The people at other table told her that they had not ordered any of the items on the tray either. Confused, Cindy returned to Matt's table and insisted that they had ordered the food which she had now been holding for several minutes. She started to argue with them, saying "I remember what you ordered and this is your food!" Furious at having been at the restaurant for nearly two hours without food, Matt could not believe that the waitress was now arguing with them about their order. He remembered that Cindy had earlier brought them their tab and quickly thought to show it to her. It was then clear that the food was not what they had ordered. Cindy went back to the kitchen and returned several minutes later, finally with their food, but it was not all there. She insisted that it was the complete order but Matt proved her wrong by showing her the tab again. Several minutes later she delivered the missing items. The entire ordeal had lasted nearly three hours.

Before leaving their table, Matt asked Cindy if she would have the manager come speak with them. They expressed their dissatisfaction to the manager, who was also the owner of the restaurant, recounting the full tale and complaining that it had taken nearly three hours to get their meal. The manager responded by saying that the server was new and he asked them to be patient with her. Matt thought that they had been patient enough and stated that he felt the manager should compensate them in some way for such an unpleasant experience. The manager replied that nothing could be done and that the party would have to pay the bill in full.

1. Why do you think this situation happened?
2. Do you think Cindy was at fault?
3. What advice might you offer to Matt?
4. What advice might you give to the manager?

Case 28

The Surprise Move

Joanne Emerson is an administrative assistant in the human resources department of The Sheldon, a 220-room hotel property in the Detroit metropolitan area. Her primary tasks involve data processing and preparing and handing out paychecks. All six employees in the human resource office report directly to Bob Simpson, the human resources manager. Joanne has an open and honest character as well as genuine concern for people. She is very committed to establishing good relationships with her superiors and her peers. She is pleased that many employees seek her advice if they have questions or problems and feels that she contributes to the overall morale of the Sheldon through these interactions.

The human resources department was located in the back of the building, near the employee entrance. It was comprised of two rooms, the outer office, approximately 20 feet by 20 feet and the inner office, approximately 12 feet by 20 feet. Mr. Simpson, the director of human resources, occupied the inner office, and Joanne's desk, two other desks, and several filing cabinets were located in the outer office. Responding to the Sheldon's open-door policy, the human resources department was among the most active parts of the back of the house, and Joanne thoroughly enjoyed the exchange that she had with hotel employees.

One morning when Joanne entered the office, she found an employee from the maintenance department removing her file cabinets, shelves, and computer. Her working material and personal belongings were piled on the floor and on the desk of the administrative assistant sitting next to her. The maintenance man, answering her question about what he was doing, informed her that he was told to move her desk to a room down the hall that was currently occupied by housekeeping supervisors. A new copy machine and printer were going to be installed where her desk had been located. He did not know who initiated the order to remove her desk. He had been assigned the job by his supervisor, who had instructed him simply to put her belongings on the floor, saying, "She's going to have enough time to organize the stuff later."

Joanne was very confused about the removal of her desk. She did not know the reasons for the change and wondered if she had done something wrong, if she was going to be terminated, if there was a conspiracy among her co-workers, or if it was perhaps just a miscommunication between the maintenance manager and his personnel. Her initial anger was directed toward the maintenance employee, whom she blamed for not taking appropriate care of her belongings.

Joanne was very upset and confronted Mr. Simpson about the situation. To her disappointment he did not show much concern for her problem. He reminded her that she had been told about the new copy machine and printer at the last staff meeting a week ago. Joanne recalled that the new equipment had been discussed; however, the location of her desk had never been mentioned in the meeting. Mr. Simpson claimed that he was "more than sorry" about any misunderstanding and inconvenience but advised her to "take it easy." He explained that the decision about where to place the equipment was made way above him.

Separated from the activity of the human resources department, and working alone in her new office, Joanne felt isolated and no longer appreciated by the organization. Interactions with other employees dwindled, as did her role as concerned listener and advisor. The activity which she most enjoyed and was proud of as a contribution that added value to the hotel disappeared with her location change. She was also suspicious of Bob's attempt to persuade her that she had been informed about the move. She was sure that the location of her desk had not been part of any meeting's discussion. Although she continued to perform her data processing and payroll functions, she lost her trust in the director of human resources and the confidence she had previously felt as a valued employee.

1. How might this situation have been avoided?
2. How might Mr. Simpson have handled the situation differently?
3. Discuss the ramifications of the move itself.

Part Six

GROUP PROCESS

We thought we were succeeding because of all the stories we heard about how hard everyone was working.

—ROBERT KENNEDY

Groups in Organizations

There are two basic types of groups in organizations, formal and informal. Formal groups are those designated by the organization and may include departments, task forces, department heads, executive committees, quality circles, and work teams. These groups typically are given a specific charge by management that will assist the organization in achieving its goals. They meet on a set schedule, document their activities, and have specific rights and responsibilities. In contrast, informal groups form in organizations primarily because of similar interests or proximity. The mechanism for control among these groups is not organizational rules and regulations but the norms that they develop for themselves. These groups can have a tremendous impact on organizational outcomes, as they may assist or frustrate the organization in achieving its goals. In an industry such as this where people, not machines or computers, do the work, understanding the informal organization can be a great asset to a manager. The formal organization chart may not accurately reflect where the truly powerful and influential people are located.

Informal leaders are selected by organizational members because they are respected, admired, and trusted. These people may be located anywhere in an organization, and they can be powerful opinion shapers. Recognizing and cultivating positive relationships with informal group leaders can be very beneficial to a manager. They can be a manager's best friend or worst enemy—it depends on the manager.

Group Dynamics

Most of you have probably worked on group projects that went extremely well. Unfortunately, most of you have probably worked on group projects that were dismal experiences, perhaps with one or two people doing all the work. What made the difference? There are three basic approaches that people might take in a group setting. First is a task orientation, where the focus is on the product of your efforts and the goal is to get it done. Second is a maintenance orientation, where the emphasis is on the process of the group, the goal being that everyone gets along and has a good time. Third is the self-orientation, where the focus is on getting your way regardless of what other people may want. The latter approach is usually dysfunctional for the group, and too much of either of the first two approaches usually results in conflict. So why do we use groups? When should we use groups? Norman Maier recognized that the use of groups provides both assets and liabilities, depending on how the process is managed. His findings are summarized below.[1]

GROUP ASSETS

Greater sum total of knowledge and information—
  more information in a group than in any of its members.
Greater number of approaches to a problem—
  people get into ruts in their thinking.
Participation in problem solving increases acceptance—
  critical factor in implementation.
Better comprehension of decision by each individual—
  mutual understanding of process and outcome.

GROUP LIABILITIES

Social pressure to conform—
  majority opinions, social desirability—who changes?
Satisficing in decision making—
  suboptimal outcome to please varied interests.
Individual domination of the process—
  false perception of leadership, compliance without
  commitment.
Secondary goal of individual group members—
  winning argument versus being right.

In short, groups should be used when the task is complex and is of sufficient size to require the labor of several people. Leadership should not be confused with control, and effective leaders in the future will be those who can facilitate a group process to maximize utilization of the available human resources. Group members need to understand that there are two important components that lead to success, good process and good product. An effective process will probably lead to a high-quality product and positive long-term group relations: a high-quality product created with a poor process will probably have negative long-term effects. Both task and maintenance orientations are needed for successful group dynamics.

Overview of the Incidents

In the following scenarios you will witness how both the formal and the informal organizations operate. You will see how group members may sanction other members for the violations of norms. These incidents reveal where the true power may exist in organizations.

Endnote

[1]Norman Maier, *Psychological Review*, Vol. 74(4), 1967, pp. 239–249.

Case 29

The Job Opening

Debbie had been the front office manager of the Limoges Hotel for six months when Judy, the assistant front office manager, left to take a job in another city. Judy had worked in the hotel since its opening four years earlier and had done an excellent job. Debbie was sorry to lose her.

When the job opening for assistant front office manager was posted, Debbie received applications from a number of people, most of whom were fairly well qualified. After reviewing all the résumés, Debbie selected the following three internal candidates for further consideration. Art had started at the Limoges Hotel as a morning front desk clerk eight months earlier. His previous experience was limited, and he had never held a full-time management position before, but Debbie had noticed his performance with customers and felt that he was extremely capable of making independent decisions. Megan, also a front desk clerk, had worked in the hotel since its opening. Megan had started in the cash office of the accounting department, received a transfer to the front desk, and through her tenure had been advanced to senior clerk. Prior to this opening, she had applied unsuccessfully for several positions in other departments of the hotel at higher managerial levels. She was hopeful for the promotion to assistant manager. Mona, a reservationist, also applied for the position. Like Megan, she had been working at the hotel longer than Art, but only by three months. Mona had previous managerial experience, having worked in an assistant manager's position at a nearby hotel and felt confident that this, combined with her error-free work as a reservationist, would enable her to secure the advancement. Debbie interviewed all three candidates and after a brief deliberation, awarded the assistant front office manager's position to Art.

Although no formal announcement of Art's promotion was made to the front desk employees, Debbie did meet separately with Megan and Mona to explain the reasons for her decision. Megan was disappointed, but having been through the process several times, seemed to accept the decision readily. Debbie's meeting with Mona, however, was more heated, as Mona disagreed with Debbie's selection and attempted to argue that she was the better candidate. Mona eventually realized that Debbie's decision was final, and left the meeting feeling shocked, outraged, and cheated. Mona reasoned that not only did she have a greater level of experience, she had worked with the hotel longer, and her performance was better than Art's. She remembered thinking during the interview that Debbie was not listening to her, and she now wondered if the decision to promote Art had already been made at that time. She was surprised that seniority had not been a consideration in this decision, as she knew it had been an important criterion in similar promotions that had been made in the hotel. Mona also questioned why the qualifications needed for the job were never made clear to all employees in the hotel. Capping all of this, it was learned that around the time of the promotion, Art had moved into the apartment building where Debbie lived. Harboring all of these suspicions, Mona effectively convinced most of the other front desk employees that Art's selection was made in an unfair and discriminatory manner and that she, in fact, should have been chosen. Along with hearing rumors that Debbie and Art were romantically involved based on his recent move, some employees tended to agree with Mona for their own reasons. Some were angry that they had not been considered for the promotion even though they applied. Others knew Art to be an outspoken person who had not built a strong rapport within the office, and therefore they did not accept him as being qualified for the job. Mona had built this rapport, so her complaints were listened to and believed. As Mona continued to bemoan her fate, the office developed increasing frustration and anger about Debbie's management practices. The reputations of both Debbie and Art were seriously affected, and the staff's respect for both of them deteriorated.

1. Is Mona right about the promotion decision?
2. What mistakes were made by Debbie?
3. What should Debbie do now to resolve the situation?

Case 30

The Suarro Inn

The Suarro Inn, located in the southwestern United States, has a wonderful geographic location, being very scenic and easily accessible by air or ground travel. Although the buildings and grounds are beautiful, the architect had little experience in designing hotels. The Suarro Inn is comprised of seven buildings separated by large areas of green space. The rather sprawling nature of the design creates many logistical problems. Six of the seven buildings are three-story residential units, each containing 100 rooms, all of which have a view of the surrounding mountains and desert. The seventh and central building contains the lobby, meeting rooms, and restaurants. The resort has 18 tennis courts, two large swimming pools, a golf course, and a fully equipped health spa. The sheer size and extent of these facilities have made them somewhat difficult to staff and they have been very costly to maintain.

The arrangement of the Suarro Inn's three restaurants, all in the main building of the complex, also pose some difficulties for the front-line employees. Two of the restaurants are served by the same kitchen but are managed separately. The third is a rooftop gourmet restaurant that has its own manager, chef, and kitchen but no dishwashing facilities. The service elevator that accesses the rooftop restaurant connects to a corridor on the ground floor that leads to the main kitchen. The wait staff entry to the banquet rooms is also off this same corridor, which is used as the primary storage area for kitchen and serving equipment as well. Further down the corridor is the housekeeping office, which contains the laundry facilities. The situation is further complicated by the labor supply, which, although plentiful, is for the most part unskilled. In addition, there are often language difficulties between management and the hourly staff.

The Suarro Inn has not been as profitable as the owners, a group of retired manufacturing executives from Detroit and Chicago, had expected. It has been running well below the 80 percent occupancy and $180 average room rate that were forecasted for the property. James Adams was hired as the new general manager one month ago to improve both the quality of operations and the level of profitability.

Deciding where to focus his attention was very difficult under the circumstances, but the housekeeping department appeared to be in the most chaotic state if not in total disarray. The former general manager, Cliff Axton, had terminated Jack LeMay, the director of housekeeping, just weeks prior to his own departure. Mr. Axton felt that even though Jack had a strong technical background, his lack of managerial experience was the cause of most of the problems in housekeeping. In his place Axton hired Oscar Hand, a knowledgeable veteran with 20 years of management experience. Oscar had a reputation of high performance with a large commercial food manufacturer. Although Oscar had never worked for a hotel, he was well versed in sanitation procedures and he had previously supervised a large custodial staff. Oscar's management philosophy was simple: Be firm, be fair, and run a "tight ship." He believed that he had to make a quick, sharp impact on his new employees to convey his "shape up" message.

Oscar felt that there were two major departmental changes that he had to make. One was to increase his control over the housekeeping staff, and the other was to reduce costs. To accomplish the first, he reorganized the structure of the department and devised a system to supervise the housekeepers closely to assure that rooms were cleaned properly. In the process he eliminated a housekeeper and assigned each of the remaining housekeepers an additional room to service. To motivate his staff, he thought it would be appropriate to establish goals, which he dictated to the housekeepers, and to provide them with feedback regarding progress toward the goals. Attacking the cost issue, he decided that the department should cut by 10 percent the use of polysorbinate, as it was very expensive cleaning agent. Finally, Oscar obtained input from his boss, the rooms division director, to determine where he should focus his attention to improve the quality of service.

As a result of this conversation, he prioritized three areas of the hotel that merited immediate attention.

Based on the goals and priorities that Oscar had developed, he assigned work teams to each of his three projects. In addition, he provided each team with a specific timetable for accomplishing various stages of his plan and assured them that he would closely monitor their progress to let them know how they were doing.

To Oscar's surprise, following all of his changes the hotel experienced a decrease in housekeeping quality of service and behavior from his staff that bordered on insubordination, especially from two supervisors, Maria Rios and Glenda Wyatt. Maria and Glenda had openly defied his demands to reduce the use of the cleaning agent as he directed. He punished Maria, issuing her three days off without pay, but found this strategy to be a near-catastrophe, as almost half of the housekeepers called in sick on the days that she was suspended. He was also plagued with the problem of often not being able to find his employees, who seemed to disappear for long periods of time. When he questioned Glenda about this, she simply replied, "It's a big place to cover and the housekeepers have to spend a lot of time walking between buildings to clean rooms and get supplies. It is not their fault that things are so spread out." Glenda also took this time with him to complain about the crowded corridor outside the housekeeping office, which all of them had to pass through every time they needed supplies. At the beginning and end of shifts it was especially difficult, as they all collided when punching the time clock. Oscar was at a loss as to what he should do, and he had just received a note on his desk calling him to the general manager's office.

1. What has caused this situation?
2. What is wrong with Oscar Hand's plan?
3. What could now be done to resolve the situation?

Case 31

Burrito Sisters

Burrito Sisters was the brainchild of Marie Shannon, a woman in her early thirties who had spent 10 years as a chef in the American southwest. Marie began with one small restaurant located just off Michigan Avenue in Chicago's business district. An emphasis on fresh ingredients, fast service, and large portions resulted in tremendous growth and quickly "The Sisters," as it soon became known, had to move to a larger location. Three years later Marie had opened six more restaurants in the Chicago area and had established corporate headquarters in a small warehouse centrally located among the seven locations.

This building provided room for offices and storage for paper products and nonperishables. Since space was at a premium in all the restaurants, Marie also set up a commissary in the warehouse, where much of the initial food preparation occurred. This allowed Maria to achieve the best and most cost-effective use of space in the seven outlets. Purchasing had also been centralized to provide Marie with leverage to negotiate bulk prices with purveyors, and every morning trucks delivered supplies from the warehouse to each of the restaurants. Given the expansion and the increasing complexity of the business, Marie had hired four professionals to help her. Janet Reed managed the commissary and food preparation, Elizabeth Nu was in charge of marketing and promotions, Shirley Mitchell was director of purchasing, and Joan Laker was the controller. There were now 20 full-time and several part-time employees working in the headquarters alone, and each restaurant also had a staff of approximately 20. Marie found herself further from operations than she wanted to be and relied heavily on her management staff. She knew that this was the cost of growth, and she wanted to continue to expand. She was confident in the ability of all four women and felt particularly good that they all shared a positive camaradie.

Joan Laker prides herself on being what she believes is a model manager, someone who is always in control of any given situation. She is extremely organized and methodical, yet highly efficient. As a manager she demands similar behavior from her staff. She is particularly pleased with the computerized accounting system she devised and implemented at Burrito Sisters. Overall she is satisfied with her employees and the department's performance, and she is comfortable in her bright, spacious corner office, but the last couple of weeks have been troublesome.

Four months earlier she had begun to have arguments with Jim Quick, her payroll clerk. Jim was experienced in his position and performed his responsibilities exceptionally well, but he had started to question various procedures, particularly the way in which she wanted specific tasks done. Joan found these encounters increasingly annoying and decided that removing Jim from the department would solve the problem. Recently, she spotted her opportunity and convinced Marie to have Jim transferred to the purchasing department, which is located in the basement next to the shipping dock. Jim, who was really well liked and respected by his co-workers in the accounting office, did not want to change departments but felt that he had no choice in the matter. Since Jim's transfer, Joan has noticed that her schedule, and her department, have been disrupted. For example, computer software that she desperately needs was ordered six weeks ago, but Shirley Mitchell, the director of purchasing, keeps telling her that it is on back order. Jim's replacement, Todd, is not learning the system as fast as she had hoped and has made significant errors. Joan had been counting on the rest of her staff to help in Todd's training, but suddenly they are following company rules, regulations, and their job descriptions to the letter. Not only are they being unhelpful with Todd, they will not go out of their way at all to assist people from other departments, even though they used to be extremely cooperative. Tensions have begun to build throughout the warehouse, and Janet and Elizabeth had called her to ask what was going on. While they had her on the phone, they also complained that payroll was not being delivered to the restaurants on time. Joan is worried not only about her department but that her professional relationships with the company are suffering, too. She wants to discuss the situation with Marie, but she has been too busy with her plans to begin franchising Burrito Sisters. Joan wants to do something but does not know what action she should take.

1. What has caused Joan's situation?
2. What suggestions might you have for her to resolve it?

Case 32

The Department Meeting

Eric Malone had recently joined the Wyatt Hotel in San Francisco as the assistant steward. He had worked summers for the past three years at various hotels near his home in Dallas, but this was his first professional job following graduation from college. The chief steward was Ralph Schaefer, a retired military officer. Ralph had been on the job several months before Eric arrived and seemed to be having some difficulty managing his staff. Scheduling was a particularly sore spot among the employees and relations between the steward and banquet departments were strained, to say the least. Ralph had called a meeting to attempt to resolve some of the problems that he felt the department was experiencing. He required that all steward department employees attend the meeting, even those who had the day off. He explained that they would be paid for the time that they attended the meeting.

At 3:00 P.M. on Tuesday the meeting began, but several employees did not show up on time. By 3:15 P.M., however, all but one of the employees were present. Ralph began the meeting by stating that things were not going as well as he expected, and the purpose of the meeting was to get some feedback and ideas from the employees for ways to "make this a better place to work." Most of the employees were surprised, but pleased, that Ralph was asking for their opinions, and the discussion started on an upbeat note.

Tyrone Jones, a veteran of several years in the steward department, began by saying, "The banquet waiters always just throw the dishes, glassware, and silver on the trays and buscarts outside the banquet rooms. This makes my job twice as hard and lots of things get broken. Judy cut her hand on a broken glass last month and had to go to the hospital for stitches." Ralph responded: "I don't want this to turn into a gripe session, I want to focus on how we can improve things in our department." Tyrone crossed his arms over his chest and pushed back slightly from the table. Judy looked at Tyrone and rolled her eyes.

Sylvia Walker, a supervisor in the department, said that she felt there were too many different kinds of stemware being used in the three restaurants the steward department served. "Some of the glasses don't fit into the glass racks for the dish machine, and we are breaking a lot of expensive glasses. Why doesn't the hotel standardize the types of glasses it uses, or at least why don't we have glass racks to fit all the glasses?" Ralph jotted her comment down, but was shaking his head as he did so.

Marvin Parks was known as a bit of a clown in the department, but he kept things moving and he made it a more enjoyable place to work with his jokes and pranks. He said, "It seems like sometimes there aren't enough of us to do the work and other times there isn't enough to do. Does anyone else feel this way?" Several people agreed with Marvin, and Bill Williams started to say something when Ralph interjected, "This is a tough business and sometimes you just don't know when things are going to get hectic." Bill, Marvin, and several others leaned back in their chairs and a silence fell over the room. "Does anyone else have any ideas?" Ralph asked.

Tyrone decided to try again but was interrupted by Barbara Lane, who said, "I just can't carry those five-gallon buckets of detergent up those narrow stairs. I always have to find someone to help me, and sometimes this really slows down the dish machines." Tyrone nodded and again leaned back in his chair. Several others leaned forward in anticipation of discussing this issue, as it affected almost all of them. Ralph replied, "I sympathize with you Barbara, but we get a much better price buying it in those buckets, so I don't think there is much we can do about that."

Tyrone again spoke up but this time did not lean forward. "Ralph, before you got here everyone would sometimes have a weekend off. I have worked here longer than most of the people in this room, but I would not mind working some weekends so that other people could have more time with their families." This comment elicited enthusiastic comments from many of the employees. Ralph looked around the room and said: "Look, people, if I try to start scheduling you on any basis other than seniority it is going to become a confusing mess. Someone will always be complaining about favoritism or something. The system is most fair just the way it is. Don't you agree?" The room again fell silent.

Ralph began to explain his ideas for improving things in the department, but the employees now were all leaning back in their chairs and barely paying attention. Eric noticed that George Ng, a dishwasher who was a Vietnamese immigrant, was trying to say something, but Ralph ignored him and kept on talking about his plans for the future. Eric had a suggestion of his own to make but kept his mouth shut. At 4:25 P.M. the meeting was concluded and Ralph thanked his employees for coming and sharing their ideas. He thought the meeting was a great success and decided to hold a department meeting the first Tuesday of every month.

1. Was this meeting as effective as Ralph believes?
2. What were the important dynamics in the situation?
3. What advice might you have for Ralph?

Part Seven

DIVERSITY IN THE INDUSTRY

*You can't expect people to see eye to eye with you
when you are looking down on them.*
—UNKNOWN

The world is changing and as the planet's population increases, the separation that we have from one another is decreasing. Social changes have led to increasing problems with substance abuse and employee depression and violence. Managers now face differences in sexual preference, the needs of the challenged, and cultural diversity. Managing in this environment demands not only a thorough understanding of the law, but also a high degree of interpersonal skill.

Along with these changes there has been an increasing focus on diversity in both customers and employees. The demands of customers are changing as they become more informed and sophisticated in their purchasing behavior. Demographic changes have had an impact on the patterns of travel and leisure spending. International travel is increasing dramatically, in both the business and leisure segments, resulting in exposure to different cultures. People are living longer, and senior citizens are placing different demands on products, services, and facilities. Accompanying changes in the consumer are changes in the workforce. As the level of education has risen, the expectations of workers has increased. In the last two decades the number of women working out of the home has doubled and the number of single parents has increased significantly, making issues such as child care more important to employees. Immigration has resulted in a large number of non-English-speaking people in the workforce. Diversity has become commonplace in the hospitality industry and will continue to do so.

Managing Differences

Conflict is the outcome of mishandled differences. Conflict is not necessarily a bad outcome and differences are natural, but you must learn to manage differences. In some instances there are legal parameters that clarify how differences must be handled. For example, Equal Employment Opportunity legislation protects certain groups of minorities, and the Occupational Safety and Health Administration (OSHA) requires that certain practices be followed. The fact that this legislation exists does not mean that it guarantees compliance. A recent survey revealed that 80 percent of male and 90 percent of female hospitality managers believe that sexual discrimination occurs frequently.[1] In many cases judgment will have to be used to resolve differences. For example, in most states there is little regulation of smoking in privately owned organizations, yet decisions about a smoking policy must be made to satisfy both internal and external customers.

Conflict usually comes in one of two types. The first is substantive, when there are differences is facts, ideas, goals, or methods. The second is affective, when there are differences in personality, values, or emotions. Substantive conflict can often escalate into affective conflict, and the latter is much more difficult to resolve. Accurately diagnosing the underlying cause of conflict is the first step toward resolving it. Once the differences are identified, efforts can be made to work toward a mutually acceptable outcome.

Overview of the Incidents

Most of you have been in arguments over trivial issues that escalated into major conflicts. Effective managers do not let this happen. Effective managers also understand the laws that impact certain groups of people, but sometimes legal compliance does not go far enough to provide a guest with a high-quality experience or an employee with a satisfying and productive work environment. In the following incidents you will see how differences from both internal and external customers were really handled in several hospitality organizations.

Endnote

[1]R. H. Woods and R. R. Kavanaugh, "Gender discrimination and sexual harassment as experienced by hospitality-industry managers," *The Cornell Hotel and Restaurant Administration Quarterly*, February 1994, pp. 16–21.

Case 33

Nancy Jones

Nancy Jones is an intelligent, exceptionally skilled, confident, and outspoken woman in her late twenties, who, by medical standards, is classified as obese. She graduated with a bachelor's degree in business marketing from a major private university and accepted a position in a management training program with a large hotel corporation, Nothill Inc., in the food and beverage area.

Nancy spent approximately one and a half years with Nothill Inc., during which time she experienced continuous conflict with her immediate supervisor, who was responsible for Nancy's performance appraisal and any promotion recommendations. It became clear that Nancy's supervisor disliked her and was not going to promote her when the supervisor announced that one of Nancy's peers would be receiving a promotion to manager of one of the hotel's several restaurants, a position Nancy had made it clear she desired. Indignant, Nancy was quick to approach the supervisor about the situation, but her response was: "You are not qualified for the position of manager." Given her education and year and a half of management training experience, Nancy felt differently about her qualifications, and immediately sought other employment.

Although disappointed with her original employer, Nancy was not completely discouraged about the hospitality industry. Although she considered the alternatives of returning to school to obtain a master's degree or trying another career field, she ultimately accepted a position in a second hotel company, in which she was looking for a chance to have more control over her career and to be treated fairly. This property, Clearview, was a 400-room convention hotel with both high occupancy and high turnover in the front office. Nancy was employed by Clearview as a front office clerk. Her strong background in computers enabled her quickly to understand the hotel's operating systems. She also really enjoyed the direct customer contact, although being the most recently hired, she was given mostly second or third shift hours during her first few weeks. After two months Nancy had proven herself to be highly competent and capable of handling the desk in the absence of any of the assistant managers. She was given a steadier workweek and scheduling preferences, and soon was asked to train new front office clerks. Nancy thought of the latter as an opportunity to exhibit her managerial capabilities and gladly accepted the additional responsibility. She had trained two new clerks successfully and found herself in demand by many of the other clerks and assistant managers on different shifts to assist with training new employees.

Although Nancy still perceived advancement possibilities stemming from these new training experiences, her hours again became haphazard and she did not receive specific time off that she requested. In addition, the front office manager no longer coordinated with Nancy as to when she would be training new employees. Instead, he simply scheduled her when he would schedule new trainees and informed the new employees that Nancy would show them everything. Nancy would find out that she was training somebody when she came in to work, not even a day in advance. Sometimes the manager asked her to come in even when she was not scheduled to train new employees. During this same period the assistant managers were leaving the desk more and taking longer breaks, announcing that she could "handle it," leaving Nancy there alone. The other clerks began to notice that Nancy was not smiling as much as she used to and that she didn't joke around with them anymore. When she finally complained to the front office manager about one of the assistant managers in particular, he told her that she probably was reading too much into the situation but that he would take care of it. The next day the assistant manager confronted Nancy and told her: "I do not appreciate you going behind my back discussing our interactions with my supervisor." A few weeks later Nancy asked the front office manager to be transferred to guest services as concierge. He denied her request, saying "You are needed at the front desk and I don't think that concierge would be appropriate for you."

Feeling that management was taking advantage of her skills without offering advancement, Nancy became increasingly withdrawn from the department, vocal in criticism of her supervisor, and uncooperative. She avoided training new employees and wouldn't assist them in correcting their mistakes. She took extended breaks and no longer exhibited her previous initiative to handle the more complex problems and situations, preferring instead to call the manager on duty, which often resulted in a delay in satisfying the needs of the guests. Nancy was reprimanded for her lack of cooperation but was still stinging with resentment at what she felt was unfair treatment by one of the assistant managers. Frustrated and on the verge of quitting, Nancy spoke with the rooms division manager. The concierge position had been filled, but Nancy was determined to be transferred out of the front office. The rooms division manager was sympathetic and asked Nancy to be patient. Eight months after her first day at Clearview she was moved to assistant housekeeping manager.

1. Was Nancy treated properly in this incident?
2. Was Nancy's behavior appropriate in this incident?
3. Do you suspect there are legal issues involved?

Case 34

The Disabled Traveler

As director of ministries for persons with handicapping positions, BettyLou Barnes flew 220,000 miles in the past year to meet with groups of disabled people. BettyLou is herself disabled, requiring a cane to assist her in walking, and is unable to climb stairs. During this time, she encountered many unpleasant situations in dealing with various airlines, most of which were merely rude and inconsiderate while some were illegal.

When BettyLou accepted this position she knew that her job would involve a lot of air travel. Prior to the circumstances that led to her disability, BettyLou had been a successful business manager and had flown frequently in her work. She felt confident in her understanding of how airports and airlines functioned and did not anticipate any problems navigating her way through terminals and aboard airplanes. In her new role as counselor for those with disabilities, she was looking forward to traveling to these people to help them in coping with their problems.

From the beginning, when BettyLou attempted to work with a local travel agent in booking her reservations, which often involved several legs and layovers, she encountered difficulties. BettyLou wanted the travel agent to have the airlines note the fact that she was disabled and to request curbside check-in and specific seating when possible. Betty-Lou found, however, that this information never seemed to be communicated by the travel agent to the airline, so she resorted to making reservations for herself.

In speaking with the airline reservations agent, BettyLou would always identify herself as a disabled person who would be needing special assistance upon arrival at the airport. She asked about walking distances in particular airports, and if any stretch was too far, she requested that a wheelchair be made available. She inquired about the plane size and seat configuration so she could request seating that would accommodate her specific needs. She found it much more convenient and comfortable to have an aisle seat directly behind the bulkhead. In most cases she was assured that her requests could be granted. In reality, they seldom were.

On one of BettyLou's trips she was still using crutches and arrived at the airport to find that she was ignored by skycaps who obviously recognized that she was having difficulty. Only after becoming quite aggressive did she receive any assistance from the skycaps, and she was still forced to stand in an awkward line waiting to have her baggage checked, which resulted in her legs being knocked and banged by the luggage of others around her. Her baggage finally checked, BettyLou walked a great distance to the ticket counter, where the agent denied any knowledge of her disability and wanted to know specifically what her problem was. After being forced to explain how she became disabled, BettyLou was then told that she should have informed the airline in advance, which she had in fact done. BettyLou was also told that her requested seat was not available, but if absolutely necessary, the steward on the plane may be able to move someone.

To proceed to her plane, BettyLou was able to get a ride on the trolley to the boarding gate, where she received yet another impression of how disabled people are treated. She was told, "The plane is very full and we can't move any passengers." She was allowed to preboard with the first-class passengers, but after making her way down the gangway she was informed by the steward: "You can't have crutches on this flight, they should have been checked." After she had made her way to her seat the steward took her crutches and said they would be returned to her after landing. He also suggested, "You should have bought a first-class ticket, then we could take care of you." BettyLou felt helpless.

Following the landing, she learned that her crutches had been stored in the exterior luggage compartment, so she could not deplane with the rest of the passengers. Without her crutches, BettyLou could not even get out of her seat. Eventually she was helped to a wheelchair that had been brought up to the side door and was transported to the terminal with the food carts. Eventually, her crutches were returned to her, but she received no apology for her inconvenience and, in fact, was treated as if she had inconvenienced the airline employees. She was wheeled to curbside, where her luggage was waiting, but this was apparently where the airline service stopped, because she was again at the mercy of the skycaps while she attempted to get a taxi to take her to her final destination.

The description above is merely of one incident of many that BettyLou has endured with commercial airlines. Often, after taking special care in making her reservations, she finds that no notice has been posted in the computer, on her ticket, or on her boarding pass about her specific needs. At the airport any knowledge of her disability was often denied and blamed on "computer error." Policies would vary from plane to plane and airport to airport even with the same airline. Access to rest rooms was, at best, difficult. Once, when walking with her cane, she was asked, "Will your Seeing Eye dog be joining you?" On flights where she had to change planes, she would often have to repeat ordeals like that described above several times in a single day.

These incidents were not unique to one airline. In the past year BettyLou wrote letters to several airlines explaining her situation and asking questions about policies for dealing with the disabled. She suggested that information regarding disabled persons be entered in the computer or that disabled persons be given some sort of identification card that would assist them in reservations, check-in, and transportation in the airport. She received no answers to her questions but did receive two form letters thanking her for her comments.

1. Why do situations such as these occur?
2. Whose responsibility was it to make BettyLou's traveling easier?
3. What could be done to prevent these types of situations?

Case 35

The Gay Co-worker

On Monday morning, Eric, the front office manager, was sitting at his desk, frustrated by the amount of work that lay ahead in the coming week. Scott, one of Eric's subordinates, knocked on his office door and requested a few minutes of his time. After a bit of small talk, Scott asked Eric if it would be possible to be transferred to the food and beverage department of the hotel. Eric was taken aback, as Scott was one of his best employees.

Eric was determined to find out the reason behind the request, as Scott had seemed to be very satisfied in his work and Eric did not like the idea of losing him to another department. Eric asked, "Can you talk to me about this? Is there anything I can do to help?" Scott was very evasive, simply stating that it was for "personal reasons." Eric continued to probe, assuring Scott that he was a valued employee whom he did not want to lose. Finally, Scott said that he had just found out that Jake, one of his co-workers, was gay. Scott explained that he is from a Midwestern town with old-fashioned values and being around Jake made him very uncomfortable. He said, "I don't understand gays and I don't want to."

Eric had known for quite some time that Jake was gay. To his knowledge, in the six months that Jake had been working in the front office, he had made no advances on any of his co-workers and he had been a model employee. He asked Scott if there was anything that Jake had done to embarrass or offend him in any way. Coldly, Scott said "No." When Eric attempted to continue the conversation noting, "You two have been friends for months, and I don't see why this should change your friendship," Scott practically spat out a reply. With disdain in his voice, Scott said he felt that Jake's sexual orientation was an abomination and that he felt personally betrayed and disgusted by their friendship. Scott was adamant that he and Jake could not work together. Although Eric knew he must return the conversation to a moderate tone, he was at this point feeling irritated by Scott's attitude. In an attempt to make Scott consider other alternatives and to feel a part of the decision-making process, Erik asked Scott if he had any suggestions about how to remedy the situation, short of a transfer. Taken by surprise, Scott responded somewhat quickly, "I really hadn't thought much about it, I just want to move to a different department in the hotel." His voice was shaky and he was noticeably nervous with this question.

Eric was going over his possible options in his head as Scott sat in front of him with his eyes looking down at the floor. Eric felt he should confront the gay issue directly and reasserted his control over the conversation by saying, "I am trying to understand your feelings of uneasiness, but there are gay employees throughout the hotel, including in food and beverage. The hotel values all types of diversity." He then suggested that Scott separate people's personal lives from the workplace, while thinking to himself that if Scott was incapable of doing that, perhaps it was Scott, not Jake, who was the problem.

Although still somewhat exasperated with Scott, Eric did not want to lose a competent employee, so he began to consider the possibility of a compromise, one that Scott would find agreeable, preferably one that Scott played a role in developing. He asked Scott point blank if he enjoyed working at the front desk. Scott replied that in fact he did enjoy his job very much. Eric again asked Scott what he thought might be some alternatives that would enable Scott to stay in a job he enjoyed while resolving his difference with Jake. Having given Scott time to think throughout the latter part of the conversation, Eric was relieved when Scott asked if there was any way that he and Jake could work different shifts, as opposed to something ridiculous like firing Jake. Eric thanked Scott for making a reasonable suggestion and agreed that the shift change was a possible solution.

Eric explained that he would have to examine the schedule to see if in fact the changes they had discussed would work. He did make it clear, however, that even if Scott and Jake no longer work together, they would have to interact at times when the staff congregates. Eric insisted that there could be no tension at these times and suggested that the three of them sit down to discuss this issue to prevent future problems from arising. His suggestions were not well received by Scott.

Although unable to change Scott's attitude about working with Jake, Eric believed that he had arrived at an acceptable solution, pending Jake's thoughts about the situation. Changing the schedule was not a problem and enabled him to retain both Scott and Jake as valuable employees.

1. Why did this situation come about?
2. Is anyone at fault?
3. What message was Eric sending with his decision?

Case 36

The North American Native Luncheon

Several years ago Sharon Whitegull joined a group of Alaskan Natives who traveled from their homes to Washington, D.C. They were scheduled to participate in a week-long program about the culture of Northern American Natives being sponsored by and held at the Smithsonian Institution. At the time, Sharon was a division director within the Alaska Federation of Natives. The ten women who accompanied her were members of various tribes in Alaska. Sharon had made many trips to New York, Los Angeles, and Washington, D.C. over the past several years, but none of the women with whom she was traveling had been to the continental United States. They were very excited about the opportunity to participate in the program, but they were also somewhat nervous about the trip.

On the second day of their visit Sharon decided to treat the women to lunch at one of Washington's finer restaurants. The morning program had run longer than anticipated, and they were not able to get to the restaurant until almost 1:30 P.M. They all entered the restaurant and Sharon approached the maître d' to request a table. The maître d' responded that lunch was no longer being served and there would not be a table ready until they began to serve dinner, at least four hours later. Sharon saw that there were still several parties eating lunch and, in fact, two men who had entered immediately ahead of them were just being seated at a nearby table. Witnessing this and noticing that the restaurant was not busy, Sharon asked to be seated at a table she saw that could accommodate her group. The maître d' responded, "As you wish, Madam," and led them to the table but did not offer menus.

After 10 minutes the women had not received any attention from the wait staff. They did not receive as much as a glass of water. They attempted to hail a waitperson but were ignored. Twenty minutes later, Sharon left the table and sought out the manager. He quickly told her that he was very busy and suggested that if they did not like the service at the restaurant, they should try elsewhere. Sharon, recognizing that she had little choice, informed her guests that the restaurant was no longer serving lunch and they got up from the table. There were no apologies offered by any of the employees of the restaurant, who simply watched the group leave. Sharon was embarrassed and extremely upset with the lack of consideration.

1. Why do situations such as this occur?
2. What other recourse did Sharon have?

Case 37

The New Travel Agent

Paulina Ross is the assistant manager of the World's Away Travel Agency in Minneapolis, Minnesota. The agency had a total of 16 employees, 12 of whom were certified travel specialists. The agency was owned by two women who had formed a partnership and started the business almost 20 years ago. They were very seldom in the office, as they spent much of their time traveling and visiting corporate clients. As a result, Paulina assumed a major role in the management of the office and had a significant amount of responsibility and autonomy. Paulina was born in Argentina and had lived many years in Europe. With this experience she was able to answer most of the questions from the other travel agents, who referred to her as an "excellent source of information." The owners have been impressed with her performance, feel lucky to have her, and compensate her quite well.

Paulina had been managing the office for several years when she was faced with a disconcerting situation. Will, one of her newer agents, had been coming into work late on occasion and often looked somewhat disheveled. Paulina suspected that he might have a drinking problem. After having been sick at work the day before, Paulina requested that he come and speak with her, but she was not looking forward to the interaction.

When Will walked into her office, Paulina smiled, shook his hand, and said "Please sit down." She thought it would be necessary to try and make him feel comfortable with her and so she came out from behind her desk, sat in a chair next to his, and casually asked him how he was doing. He responded with a discussion of how much he had been going out and enjoying his new life in Minneapolis. He then joked that sometimes it was "a drag to come into work." While his attitude assured Paulina that Will was at ease with her, she was also somewhat troubled by it. His response prompted Paulina to ask if Will was enjoying his job. He said, "Yeah, everything is fine." Realizing that the conversation was not going as she had planned, Paulina attempted to establish a more professional atmosphere and to reassert herself as Will's superior by inquiring if he was curious as to why she had asked him to come to her office. He said, "No."

Paulina had hoped that their conversation would clear a path for her to express her concerns, and even though it had failed, she was determined to address the issue. She began by saying, "I have noticed that you have been late for work several times in the last few weeks." When Will offered no explanation, Paulina continued, commenting that she was concerned about his job performance, and that she had heard that he had been sick in the employee lounge the day before. At the mention of the latter, Will immediately became defensive and stated, "It was blown way out of proportion." He did not try to make excuses, however, as Paulina had expected he would. She then asked him to tell her in his own words what had happened, since she had only heard about it through the grapevine. He then admitted to having had a few drinks the night before but claimed, "That was all, no big deal." Paulina was pleased but quite surprised by his honesty. When she asked him how often this occurred, however, Will again became evasive and slightly defensive, saying, "What I do on my own time is my business." Paulina then expressed to Will that his work was being affected by his personal time. To her astonishment, he dropped his defensive posture and seemed to take a genuine interest in hearing about his work.

Wanting to capitalize on this change of attitude, Paulina praised him by saying that she had been impressed by his ability and potential when she had hired him, and she believed him to be an asset to the organization. She then criticized his recent performance noting that some of his work had been turned in late with errors, adding that both his co-workers and customers were being affected. Reacting defensively to her comments, Will began to make excuses. He said that he was from the West Coast and found it hard to make friends in Minneapolis. When he did meet people, he drank "to socialize and fit in with them." Finally he stated accusingly, "I didn't know that you were going to monitor my social life!"

In an effort to calm him, Paulina assured him that she did not intend in any way to control or regulate his time outside the office. She repeated that the reason for having the meeting was that she was truly concerned about him, his job performance, and his ability to succeed with the company. It was then that he said, "I may be drinking too much, but I don't want to lose my job because of it." Paulina was relieved that the admission had come from him, and that she did not have to accuse him of excessive drinking. She was optimistic that together they could work to find a solution.

1. Evaluate the way Paulina handled the situation.
2. What would you suggest would be an appropriate course of action?

Part Eight

SEXUAL HARASSMENT

Whether the harassment takes the form of a risqué joke or a more violent form such as repeated inappropriate touching of another's body, all sexual harassment, whether intentional or otherwise, is aggression against another person's body or psyche, using sex as a weapon.

—JULIA LIGHTLE [1]

Sexual harassment has, unfortunately, become reported with increasing frequency in many hospitality organizations today. It is not clear whether this is the result of a greater propensity to report harassment, or there are actually more cases of harassment, but there are major legal, ethical, and economic concerns surrounding the issue. Many hospitality organizations operate 24 hours a day, including weekends and holidays. People often are not in what might be considered "normal" routines, and this environment requires special attention with respect to sexual harassment.

Sexual harassment is considered to be an illegal form of sexual discrimination under Equal Employment Opportunity Commission guidelines. The term refers to unwelcome sexual advances, requests for sexual favors, and inappropriate verbal or physical contact. Specifically, sexual harassment occurs under any of the following circumstances:

- Submission to the conduct is either explicitly or implicitly a term or condition of an individual's employment.

- Submission to or rejection of such conduct by an individual is used as the basis for employment decisions affecting that individual.
- Such conduct has the purpose or effect of unreasonably interfering with an individual's work performance or creating an intimidating, hostile, or offensive working environment.

Even with these standards, sexual harassment can be a gray area. Jokes that may seem inoffensive to some may be offensive to others. What may appear to be harmless flirting may in fact be harassment. A compliment about someone's attire or physique may also be perceived as harassment. The bottom line is that any sexual behavior that threatens the comfort, safety, or security of individuals may be interpreted as sexual harassment. It may occur among employees, but also between customers or guests and employees. A recent survey of hospitality managers revealed that 65 percent of female respondents believed women in this industry had been subjected to sexual harassment in the workplace.[2]

To protect employees from sexual harassment, several actions must take place. Top management must lead by example to demonstrate that sexual harassment will not be tolerated. A clear policy must be established and communicated to all employees. All complaints must be handled quickly and effectively. The message that is communicated must be clear and consistent to assure that all employees understand the seriousness of this issue. The costs involved with sexual harassment include not only potential lawsuits of both the offending organization and individual, but also the costs of turnover, absenteeism, decreased performance, and reduced morale. Most important, sexual harassment is degrading and embarrassing to the victim, who often will be hesitant to report the incident but will still suffer the consequences.

Overview of the Incidents

Hopefully, most of you have not experienced sexual harassment, but it is likely that you know someone who has. The following scenarios describe situations involving people just like yourselves, their reactions, and the action that the organizations took in response to the incidents.

Endnotes

[1]Julia Lightle, "Sexual Harassment," *Executive Housekeeping Today,* May 1992, pp. 12–13.

[2]Robert H. Woods and Raphael R. Kavanaugh, "Gender Discrimination and Sexual Harassment as Experienced by Hospitality Industry Managers," *Cornell Hotel and Restaurant Administration Quarterly,* February 1994, pp. 16–21.

Case 38

A Case of Harassment

Martha Crosby, single and in her early twenties, is a front desk clerk at a luxury hotel in Hartford, Connecticut. According to Martha's co-workers and superiors, she is "a terrific worker and a joy to work with," evidenced even further by having been chosen as an employee of the month. While working at the hotel, Martha began dating the night auditor, Jim, a 22-year-old single man. They continued dating for six months, at which time Martha broke off the relationship only to find herself being stalked and verbally abused by Jim. As a form of harassment, he called her at least six times in an eight-hour shift, every shift she worked. Martha always responded simply by hanging up. After two weeks of persistent calls, which were deliberate attempts to interrupt her work, Jim started showing up at the hotel hours before he was scheduled so as to confront Martha publicly at the front desk. He often derided her to other employees. He followed her to her car and threatened her on several occasions.

Jim continued to harass Martha for six months, during which time she attempted to ignore his behavior and pretend that she was not being affected by his malicious actions. It seems as if she was denying the situation even to herself, although Martha remembers thinking at the time that she was responsible for "getting herself into this mess" and that she must be responsible for resolving it without involving her superiors. Consequently, when Jane, the front desk manager, asked about the phone calls and the comments being made, Martha quickly changed the subject as if to say "I had not really noticed." Martha sensed that upper management would want to ignore the possibility of sexual harassment at their hotel, choosing instead to think that those types of things do not happen at a four-star preferred property. The company did not even have a stated policy on sexual harassment. Knowing this,

Martha did not think the hotel would be supportive in finding a recourse for her problem even if she did confide it to someone in management. Instead, Martha tried to avoid Jim as much as possible. She kept the doors locked to the office, she never walked to the parking lot alone, and she hung up on him each time he called. She did her absolute best to keep him from affecting her work. However, Jim's behavior did not go unnoticed and the evening shift supervisor, Sarah, began intervening with Jim's phone calls, admonished him to stop calling and to leave Martha alone. When the calls continued and he proceeded to show up at work early enough to encounter Martha, Sarah started letting Martha out early so as to miss him. As a concerned manager, Sarah tried to get Martha to talk about the situation, but Martha remained reluctant to do so. Sarah did what she could to help, without knowing exactly what the details were, and after a few weeks she finally spoke with Jane to let her know what had been occurring during the swing shift. Jane's only response was "Well, she shouldn't have dated him in the first place."

Sarah then proceeded to go over Jane's head and spoke with Doug, the rooms division manager. He told Sarah that he would look into the situation, although his initial response was similar to Jane's, commenting that Martha had gotten herself into the mess. Doug did speak with John, the controller, since night auditors fall under his supervision. John, however, did nothing.

The entire situation finally reached its climax on Memorial Day weekend when Jim decided once again to approach Martha. Since the hotel was very slow that day and Martha was covering the desk alone, she locked the door to the office so as not have to be concerned with Jim bothering her. When Jim got to the door and found it locked, he went to the lobby and jumped over the desk. He physically threatened her, and his screaming drew the attention of the two bellmen who forcibly removed him from the property.

Following this incident, Martha's supervisor Sarah went to Mary, the director of human resources and finally got a proactive response. Mary said that she was shocked at what was happening and even more disappointed that this was the first that she had heard of it. After Sarah had described the entire course of events, Mary called Doug into her office, asked Sarah to repeat the entire series, and insisted that Doug speak with Jim about his actions. Doug was to let Jim know that if he did not change his behavior, he would be let go.

1. Why did Martha handle the situation as she did?
2. Could management have done anything to help her?
3. Do you think there should be a policy prohibiting the dating of co-workers?

Case 39

The Good Dishwasher

Alexa is a college student who works part-time as a waitress at a restaurant in a university town. Like many other female servers at the restaurant, Alexa has been the victim of sexual harassment. She has been faced repeatedly with both verbal abuse and the unwanted physical contact of a co-worker, Fred, a 24-year-old dishwasher. Fred is married and the father of a small child. It is common for Fred to make crude and suggestive remarks in the presence of the female servers or to sing phrases from songs with distinct sexual overtones. He has made direct comments as to his desire for various servers, with statements such as, "One day you will be in bed with me." In addition to the verbal harassment, Fred has physically approached servers and slapped them with his hand on their rear ends. Fred slapped Alexa once, and she, fed up and furious, yelled a warning for him never to touch or speak to her again. She found herself emotionally drained by his daily assaults to the extent that she dreaded going to work because his presence made her tense and miserable. Her defense had been to ignore him; however, after she reprimanded him for slapping her, Fred modified his behavior, being pointedly complimentary with comments such as, "Alexa, your hair looks nice today."

Although Alexa was able to achieve some relief from Fred's harassment by confronting him, others on the wait staff were still being subjected to his perverse behavior. Alexa feels that she is better able to tolerate Fred's harassment because he is in a lower position than she is and because he has no authority over her. However, if he had been her superior, such behavior would have prompted her to quit or file charges.

Fred invites servers to go out with him and he was successful in actually having an affair with a server not too long ago. However, when the server wished not to see him anymore, Fred began to stalk her. He would show up at places she went and would spy on her. He has even thrown empty bottles at the server's home in the middle of the night.

Alexa spoke with other servers about the serious nature of the situation. Although the female servers were not comfortable in their current work environment, they were still reluctant to speak to management because they felt uneasy discussing the sexual nature of the problem. Alexa was the first server to bring the situation to the manager's attention. The manager, Don, has two female assistant managers who also oversee the restaurant operation. Fred's behavior, which included crazed rantings, was far worse when Don was not working and one of the female assistants was in charge. After Alexa spoke with Don, other female servers approached him with their grievances and stories of harassment. He explained to them how difficult it was to get good dishwashers and expressed his concern about the financial support of Fred's wife and child, but promised that he would do something about the situation.

Within several days, Don responded to the servers' complaints by taking Fred off night shifts when the women managers oversaw the operation. Don told Fred that the reason for the change in his work schedule was because a few servers "did not like him." Alexa usually works the night shifts, but she also works during the lunch hour a few times a week, so she still comes into contact with Fred. He seems to be a bit more subdued during the times when Don is around, but his antics have continued.

1. Why is Fred's behavior tolerated?
2. What action would you suggest to resolve the situation?

Case 40

The Assault

Sally was a young woman from Indiana who had just completed her junior year in college and had accepted a summer job as an intern at Pelican Ridge, a large resort on Hilton Head Island in South Carolina. This was Sally's first experience living so far from home, as well as her first time on the island. The move was made easier by the fact that the resort secured nearby housing and provided excellent meals for the summertime help, an arrangement with which Sally was pleased. She knew no one ahead of time from the property except John, another intern from her college.

Toward the end of her first week, Sally was working in the lounge as a waitress and ran into John for the first time since coming to Hilton Head. He seemed very happy to see a familiar face and asked her to stop by his room to talk after she got off work. He was staying in the hotel temporarily because there had been some confusion about his housing arrangements. She agreed and said she would be there in about an hour. When she finished her shift, she told her co-worker Brian that she was going to visit John, explaining that he was someone she knew from college and that she thought they would be comparing their experiences. Brian, who lived in the same apartment complex, had agreed to give Sally a ride home and she asked him to meet her at John's room when he was ready to leave. Brian's shift was also ending and he said he would come and get her in 15 minutes or so.

John met Sally at the door of his room, invited her in, and asked her to sit down. She had settled herself on the small sofa and was starting to say thank you when she noticed that John was still at the door and that he had locked it. Before she could complete her sentence, or question the door being locked, John crossed the room, sat next to her, and began kissing her. Startled, it took her a moment to react, but then she attempted to push him away. While struggling against him, she told him to stop kissing her and to let go of her. John refused and ordered Sally to "shut up." When she continued to resist him physically and verbally, he slapped her hard across the face, grabbed her by her arms and threw her down on the floor. He then tore her uniform open and began to sexually assault her. It was then that Brain arrived and knocked on the door. Not realizing who was there, John barked "go away," but Sally called Brian's name. Having heard sounds of a struggle when he approached the door, Brian refused to leave without Sally, and John finally let go of her. She ran to the door and slipped out of the room obviously shaken. Brian asked her to explain what had happened, but Sally shook her head, attempted to cover herself, and asked Brian to take her directly home. Although he agreed, he was confused as to what had actually happened. He knew from their earlier conversation that Sally wasn't going up to John's room for romantic reasons, and he saw that her clothes had been torn.

On the way home, Brian encouraged Sally to talk and she revealed what had occurred. Brian believed that she should report the incident to the general manager, but Sally felt so embarrassed and ashamed by what had happened that she was reluctant to discuss it with her superiors. Brian was persistent and after pleading with her, she finally agreed to call the general manager from her apartment.

After speaking with Sally, the general manager summarily fired John and sent him home without further questioning of John's behavior. However, an investigation did follow, for record-keeping purposes, Sally was told, that required Sally to repeat the circumstances and the result of the evening several times to the general manager. She was called from her job on more than one occasion to recount the situation, even though she had described the incident in great detail to him previously. She found these sessions with the general manager very stressful not only in repeating the events of the attack but also in answering his personal questions each time about her dating history and whether she had any prior involvement with John. He also asked her what she had been wearing at the time and to recall and recite exactly what they had said to each other before, after, and during the incident. All of these questions were quite embarrassing for Sally and put her very much on the defensive.

Rumors spread rapidly through the hotel's grapevine regarding the investigation. Sally found her story and her reputation at Pelican Ridge to be in question, as, before he left, John had claimed to a number of people that Sally had charged him falsely. Some employees were skeptical, as they had seen her speaking with John in a friendly manner earlier in the evening before the incident. Others resented the amount of time that she was away from her job and with the general manager.

Intimidated and alone, Sally endured the general manager's scrutiny and the effects of the rumors for the rest of the summer. Having the work experience that the internship provided was an important aspect of her college curriculum, so she did not confide in her family or friends at home for fear that they would pressure her to quit. While she was relieved that John was no longer working at Pelican Ridge, she couldn't help resenting the fact that he wasn't actually punished for what he had done, and she wondered if criminal charges should perhaps have been brought against him. Although somewhat vindicated when it was later learned that John was addicted to steroids and was admitted to a drug rehabilitation program, Sally felt that her relationship with many co-workers was irreversibly damaged by the many rumors about the incident.

1. Why did this situation occur?
2. Evaluate the managerial response to the incident.
3. Why did Sally's co-workers respond as they did?

Case 41

She's My Type

As the general manager of the Dixon Hotel in San Francisco, Mrs. Jones is one of very few minority women to hold such a high position in a luxury hotel in the United States. She is of Filipino descent and graduated with a bachelor's degree in hotel management 18 years ago. Mrs. Jones has devoted all of her adult life to the hospitality industry both within the United States and internationally. She recently took an attractive offer with a management company to revive the Dixon Hotel from its current debt crisis and inefficient operation.

Being a minority woman, she has found it a struggle throughout her professional life to gain respect, credibility, and equal treatment from her colleagues, employees, and superiors. A believer in equal opportunities and an activist for the cause, her journey has been particularly difficult. Prior to taking the job at the Dixon, Mrs. Jones had been the general manager of a large hotel in Los Angeles, where she was faced with a dilemma when her sales and marketing director resigned from the job. Mrs. Jones, together with the vice-president of human resources for the management company that was then her employer, conducted several interviews with potential candidates. Following are excerpts from two conversations between the vice-president and Mrs. Jones's secretary, Jill, which took place after the interviews.

Conversation 1: (After interviewing a male candidate)

VP: *See that guy over there? He's really quite a hotshot. I was really impressed with his résumé and qualifications. I hope you're not offended, Jill, that he's a man and all, but you know, I think men are better suited for the sales and marketing position.*

JILL: *What does being a man have to do with this? Why don't you think a women could do just as good a job?*

VP: *Well, I think that male sales directors are better able to handle the pressures from different constituents. Sometimes they have to be a little more aggressive and forceful in their dealings.*

Conversation 2: (Next day, after interviewing a female candidate)

VP: *I like her qualifications, she seems very competent, but we're not going to hire her. Keep her résumé on file, though, she's my type.*

JILL: *What do you mean?*

VP: *Well she's blond, which I personally like, and more mature. With older women you don't have to deal with all the problems, like pregnancy and family, that younger women have.*

After these short conversations with the vice-president, Jill was furious, and she described the situation to Mrs. Jones. Knowing the all-white-male executive board of the management company, Mrs. Jones was not surprised by the vice-president's comments. She not only understood what a problem this presented in terms of the attitude of the human resources department, but also that this practice could bring about severe legal consequences. Therefore, she decided to speak directly to the president of the management company with the hope of improving the situation. The president promised her that he would speak to the vice-president and rectify the situation, but he never followed through with his commitment.

A few weeks later, Mrs. Jones resigned from her job as the general manager. Although her reasons for resigning were complex, they stemmed mostly from differences in leadership styles, both in philosophy and conduct, as the conversations between the vice-president and her secretary illustrated. Although originally confident that she had become the general manager because of her competence, she recognized the lack of company support and saw that her opinions were not taken seriously by the executive board. Mrs. Jones believed that remaining the general manager under the authority of this particular management would have compromised her integrity, her convictions, and her values. One day after her resignation, the rooms division director, the food and beverage director, and the controller all resigned from their jobs as well.

1. Why did this situation come about?
2. Who is ultimately responsible?
3. What are some of the real and potential costs of this incident?

Part Nine

STAFFING AND PROMOTION

*All people want to succeed. Some want to succeed
so badly that they are willing to work for it.*
—UNKNOWN

If you ask low- or middle-level managers in the hospitality
industry how they spend their time, most will complain that
interviewing prospective employees takes up way too much of it.
If you delve into this issue a bit further, you will hear complaints
about turnover, accompanied by comments such as, "I just can't
get good people." The high degree of turnover in the industry
makes continuous interviewing and selection a necessity for many
managers. The question then might be asked: What causes the
turnover? Few managers would place the blame on themselves,
and the industry accepts the high levels of turnover as a given.
Turnover is the enemy of quality. It requires tremendous expenditures of time and money for recruiting, interviewing, and training. All of these activities distract a manager from managerial
tasks and result in declines in guest service. And the best people
can always leave because they will have options.

Selection is one of the most powerful tools that a manager
possesses. Research has shown, however, that managers make
hiring decisions in as little as 4 seconds into the interview process.
You wouldn't even be able to get out the "good" in "Good

morning" and the decision could already be made. One of the primary reasons this happens is that managers tend to hire people like themselves, with similar backgrounds, cultures, and even looks. They do not necessarily do this on purpose, however; they just may not know how to select the appropriate people.

To make a good selection decision, the manager must be familiar with and have information about the job for which he or she is hiring. Ideally, this would include a job description, which describes in detail the tasks involved with any position. In addition, the manager should have a job specification that details the knowledge and abilities necessary to perform a job. The manager must also have a thorough understanding of EEO legislation regarding affirmative action and protected groups to comply with federal legislation. Finally, the manager should be trained in interviewing skills to avoid making attribution errors such as the first-impression error mentioned earlier.

In many cases the selection process involves a promotion, where substantial information about the candidates' performance has been collected. It would seem that this would be easier than initial selection, yet often, the same errors are made. Employees may have a different perception of who is qualified to perform a particular job. If performance and selection criteria are not clearly understood or the promotion decision is not perceived to be fair and equitable, the decision may result in negative consequences.

Overview of the Incidents

The following scenarios provide you with several different examples of staffing decisions in hospitality organizations. These decisions send important messages through the organization and may have a major impact on motivation and satisfaction. As you read these incidents, think about how you might have done things differently.

Case 42

The Promotion Decision

Donna Hopkins is director of front office operations at a renowned luxury hotel in New York City. Her job responsibilities include managing the front desk, reservations, bellstand, and concierge both in the main lobby and on the exclusive concierge floor. Ms. Hopkins has a college degree in marketing, has over 10 years of hotel experience, and has been with the corporation for seven years. She has been in her current capacity at the hotel for four years. Throughout her seven-year tenure, Donna has done an excellent job in all of her positions and has climbed steadily in the ranks of the corporation. As part of her career progression, she is anxious to move to the executive level, and believes that she is well qualified to do so.

Upon taking the position as director, Donna found the front office to be in a state of turmoil, with excessive guest complaints and a high degree of turnover. Businesspeople, for whom timeliness and quick service are essential, account for approximately 55 percent of this hotel's clientele and room sales. Donna instituted training and quality assurance programs that resulted in greater levels of satisfaction for both guests and employees. Jonathan Bryant is the executive housekeeper of the same hotel. He has worked in various capacities in the corporation over the past 11 years and has held his current position for four years. He supervises a staff of well over 100 employees and is ultimately responsible for keeping the entire hotel spotless, as demanded by the hotel's business clientele. He has been an exemplar employee both in his technical ability and in his relations with his subordinates, which is reflected in high productivity and extremely low turnover in the housekeeping department. He, too, believes that he is ready for a promotion. Ms. Hopkins and Mr. Bryant are good friends, and they have great respect for each other's abilities.

Several weeks ago, Ms. Hopkins was faced with a situation that jeopardized the daily operation and reputation of the hotel. A large convention of attorneys was scheduled to take place in the hotel over the weekend, and the front desk staff thought they were fully prepared to handle the large afternoon crowds. On Friday at about one o'clock in the afternoon, the computer registration system of the hotel was rendered inoperable by a sudden power surge. All reservations and records of current guests were inaccessible. Guests waiting to check out or check in would have to be delayed until the system was operational.

Ms. Hopkins's response to the computer collapse was immediate. She first contacted Mr. Bryant to gain access to the housekeeping room charts to determine which rooms were available and which were occupied. She and the resident manager created a short list of rooms that should be given to the attorney group based on their room availability status and the preliminary list of rooms that they had allocated to the group in the signed contract. These lists were placed on a large room rack at the front desk for easier visibility. By coordinating with housekeeping, front desk agents were provided with new lists as soon as one list had been finished.

During this time, Ms. Hopkins instructed the front desk agents to keep clear records of all check-ins in order to place the accounts in the computer when the system was operational. Departing guests were offered the choice of direct billing or, if they chose to wait, a complimentary lunch at the luxury restaurant at the hotel. The general manager led the guests to the restaurant, informed the staff of the present situation, and instructed them simply to charge the meals to the front office/rooms division. Ms. Hopkins also instructed one of the two concierges in the lobby to assist the lobby monitors in keeping the new arrivals in neat lines and in providing them with guidance. She also received some volunteer assistance in checking in guests from the resident manager.

The general manager contacted the engineering department and instructed them to locate the source of the problem and restore the computer as soon as possible, which they did an hour and a half after the shutdown. It was discovered that an influx of electrical current from the outside had caused the damage and the hotel was one of many buildings in a five-block radius that had been so affected.

When computer service was restored, Ms. Hopkins collected all the check-in information and had employees begin to enter the data into unoccupied computers in the reservations office. After this was done they would begin to take care of the checkouts. She also contacted the restaurant and informed the staff to notify guests who would be checking out that they could proceed to the front desk. The situation had finally calmed down by four o'clock in the afternoon and they were ready for the heavy evening check-in of attorneys.

Upon arrival at the hotel on the following Monday morning, both Ms. Hopkins and Mr. Bryant were informed by the general manager that the position of executive director of the rooms division at the Chicago property had become available. Although he would be sorry to lose either one of them, the GM encouraged each of them to apply, as he felt they both deserved a promotion. Each did apply for the job with no sense of hostility between them. Two weeks after applying, they found that there were 11 applicants who had been determined to be possible candidates for the position, and they both were among them. A short list of five would be identified within the next few days. They then found that they had both made the list. Although not formally announced, it was rumored that also on the list were a manager from another hotel within the corporation, a person from a competitor, and a person from the corporate office. Over the past several months the corporate office was going through a major restructuring to reduce costs and become more efficient.

Within the next week both Ms. Hopkins and Mr. Bryant were flown to Chicago to interview with the GM and the corporate director of human resources. Ms. Hopkins felt that her interview had gone extremely well and was guardedly optimistic about getting the position. The week after her interview Ms. Hopkins found out that the position had been offered to the person from the corporate office, who was a finance specialist with very little operations experience. In her frustration she contacted her GM to try to learn more about the decision. The GM was very disappointed but explained that the corporation was trying to outplace the best corporate people into operations to retain their talent. That afternoon Ms. Hopkins called a headhunter who had contacted her off and on over the last couple of years.

1. Evaluate Ms. Hopkins's performance in the crisis.
2. Was this a good decision on the part of the corporation?
3. What message is being sent by this decision?
4. What are some of the possible costs of this decision?

Case 43

Spas International

Rex Smith had gone back to his alma mater in February to interview candidates for a position with the accounting division of Spas International (SI), a management corporation that owned and/or managed 60 luxury health clubs. Although Rex was a marketing specialist, SI made it a practice to send their executives to their old schools to recruit.

Polly White was interviewed by Rex, and the two seemed to hit it off quite well, as they had a lot in common. As a result of their conversation, Polly was offered a plant trip to SI corporate headquarters, where she was wined and dined extravagantly. The corporate controller was also impressed by Polly and offered her a position with SI, which she accepted. Polly was given her choice of several cities in which to locate, but it was suggested that opportunities were greatest in the smaller spas because of greater responsibility and visibility. On Monday, June 15, Polly began work in Tucson, Arizona.

She had been very impressed by Rex Smith and her trip to Chicago, and she was looking forward to beginning her new career. Her appearance on the first day of her job, however, surprised her new boss, who was not even aware that she was coming. "Those people at headquarters are so disorganized, they drive me crazy," he muttered, and assigned Polly to a menial task, giving her very vague instructions.

The next day as Polly arrived at work her boss told her to "make some order out of these overdue corporate account files and get in touch with those that are out over 60 days. I'm going out of town until Thursday." Polly was appalled by the archaic manual filing system in use, but she did the best she could, putting the files in alphabetic order and ordering the invoices in each file chronologically. On Wednesday she called to set up appointments for the following week with six firms whose accounts were 60 days overdue, explaining that the purpose of the visit was to establish a repayment schedule for the overdue accounts. It took a lot of work and a lot of nerve to call these people, and Polly was very proud of herself when she left for her apartment Wednesday night.

Polly arrived at the office early Thursday morning, but her boss was already there. She explained eagerly what she had done, but by the look on his face she knew something was wrong. "I can't visit accounts next week, we're receiving new equipment on Monday and most of those other days I'm tied up too. Didn't you even look at my desk calendar? And another thing, we don't establish a repayment schedule; we pick up a certified check or go directly to the Better Business Bureau. If you aren't sure about something, ask me. You youngsters have no common sense. I don't know what they are teaching you. So damned dependent on computers that you can't even think. You're even worse than the last girl they sent me." Polly was devastated.

1. How did this situation come about?
2. How could it have been prevented?
3. Who is at fault in this situation? Why?

Case 44

The Reassignment

Angela has worked in the Lamonde Cafe, one of five restaurants in a large hotel, as a waitress/prep cook for more than a year. She has enjoyed her job and has performed well in her position and was considered by her supervisor, Mr. Tracy, to be a competent and reliable worker. Mr. Tracy was particularly pleased that Angela, unlike some of the other waitresses, rarely complained about the early hours and long days. To support her family, Angela has to work. As a mother of three, she actually prefers the early morning hours as they enable her to be home by the late afternoon when her children return from school. She was thankful to have this job, not only for financial reasons, but because of its convenient location and early morning hours.

When Angela came in to work one morning, she went to the locker room to change into her uniform. As usual, her co-workers were gossiping, but this time the talk revolved around Angela. She was told that her boss had decided to move her to another department, where she would be preparing and serving employee meals. Supposedly, this change was due to overstaffing problems at the cafe. Not wanting to lose the position of waitress/prep cook in the cafe, Angela was quite concerned as she set about her work in the kitchen.

That afternoon Mr. Tracy made an appointment to talk to Angela in his office. He told Angela that he too had heard the rumors of her dismissal from the cafe, but not to worry, for they were all false. Angela's fears subsided when he joked casually with her, wondering out loud where the rumors had begun.

The next morning, again in Mr. Tracy's office, Angela was told of her transfer to the position of serving employee meals. Stunned, Angela asked for an explanation, but Mr. Tracy did not discuss the reason for the transfer, nor did he mention or apologize for his false assurances from the day before. Without further consideration, Angela was given a new job description and work area, different responsibilities, and later hours. Although her base salary remained the same, she was no longer in a position to receive tips.

Angela reported to her new division confused and angry. Due to the fact that Angela depended on her job to support her family, she felt that she had no choice other than to learn her new role and responsibilities, but her motivation and interest in the job were very low. The fact that the position required her to work past four o'clock and sometimes into the evening was very difficult for Angela, as she missed being with her children, and had to make separate arrangements for their care. The quality of her work, and the quality of the employee meals, began to decline.

1. Evaluate Mr. Tracy's behavior in this situation.
2. What are some of the potential costs of this decision?

Case 45

The Reinstatement

Tom Beene had been the manager of food and beverage at the Birdwood Inn for 18 months. During this time he had made many positive changes within the department, although some of his decisions had a negative impact on certain employees. Specifically, he had found it necessary to demote the equipment director, John Sullivan, who in his two years in the position had supervisory authority over the entire dishwashing staff of the hotel. Mr. Beene reassigned that responsibility to a kitchen staff supervisor, Ed Ackridge.

All of the dishwashers were happy with Ed's appointment as supervisor. Ed created permanent schedules, allowed the workers to complete their tasks with a minimum of supervision on his part, and held periodic meetings with all his staff. Under Ed's direction, the department seemed to flourish. Cliff, one of the dishwashers, reported that it seemed as if fewer accidents occurred on the job and everyone seemed to complain less. In essence, their new boss took his workers' needs into consideration and treated them with respect. He allowed the dishwashers to monitor their own work flow and asked them for their suggestions when determining peak times for regular dish washing service and deep cleaning in the kitchens.

Following several months of conflict with the union, Tom Beene resigned. The food and beverage department then underwent a period of upheaval that resulted in the adjustment of many positions in the department. Prior to his resignation it was rumored that Mr. Beene had planned to fire John Sullivan. After he left, however, John was reinstated to his former position as equipment director and again assumed control over the dishwashing staff.

Most of the dishwashers were dissatisfied with John's reappointment as their supervisor, particularly Cliff, who does not feel John should have ever held a supervisory position. Cliff's belief that the majority of promotions at the hotel are seniority based rather than contingent on managerial skills, job knowledge, or organizational skills was confirmed when John was reinstated. The dishwashing staff was again demoralized by the return to the chaotic schedules and autocratic demands that had characterized John's previous supervision. Although Cliff was unhappy with the situation, he felt powerless within the organization to change it. Without the support of someone such as the previous food and beverage manager, Cliff dismissed the idea of filing a grievance with the union, as he did not think it would be effective.

Instead of filing a grievance, Cliff attempted to talk to John about the situation and to explain how well the dishwashers had been performing with permanent schedules. John brushed over the complaint but said that he would look into the matter. The next posted schedule had irregular hours for all the dishwashers. Cliff was scheduled for three different shifts, often with eight hours or less between work assignments. Not wanting to appear belligerent with John, Cliff decided to work the hours as posted for the next several weeks and not complain.

Cliff knew his work process very well and took pride in his performance. Less than a month after John's reappointment, he noticed that more breakage occurred on his shifts and he was more likely to slip on the slick kitchen floor. Cliff again approached John to discuss his observations and to ask him to readjust the schedule. Similar to their first encounter, John told him that he would look into it. Cliff was accustomed to working during the third shift and deep cleaning at that time because there was little activity in the kitchen. Although still responsible for the deep-cleaning function, John scheduled him from 2 P.M. to 10 P.M. when the kitchen staff was still preparing meals. Cliff's work was constantly interrupted and the kitchen was not as clean as it once was.

Cliff's frustration led him to complain to John more strenuously. The two of them had a shouting match at work when the next schedule was posted. Cliff felt that John was not listening to him or the rest of the dish machine operator staff.

Feeling thwarted in his attempts to resolve his problems through John, Cliff approached the human resources director, Ron Cole, and explained the entire situation. Describing his own experience, Cliff noted the problems that have resulted, both at work and home, from John's erratic scheduling of the DMO staff. Cliff reported that he frequently worked three different shifts within one week, some less than eight hours apart, and that he was often unable to get more than three hours of sleep a night. Chronically fatigued he has had more breakage on the job, and has noticed a decrease in his overall performance. Cliff had also become irritable at home and his wife had told him that he has been short-tempered with his children.

Ron offered to discuss the situation with John but could not promise any results. Although Cliff's problems remained unresolved, Ron was happy that the staff was finally coming back to the human resources office with their problems rather than just filing grievances with the union.

1. Is seniority the best criteria for making staffing decisions?
2. Evaluate the effect on morale, and the reasons for it, after John's return as a supervisor.
3. What are the other costs involved with this decision?

Case 46

The Surprise Promotion

Lee Jones had been working in the front office of the Simon Hotel for almost two years. He had started right out of college as a front desk clerk and had progressed rapidly through the positions of cashier, reservations clerk, and night auditor to become a front desk supervisor. Lee was extremely well liked by everyone, and he was viewed by both his superiors and subordinates as being very competent. He usually worked about 45 hours per week and generally enjoyed his job, although recently his wife had given birth to twins girls, and balancing his private and work time had become more complicated.

One Friday afternoon it seemed as if his fellow employees were acting somewhat odd, and around 4:00 P.M., the front office manager, Sue, asked him to join her in one of the first-floor meeting rooms. Opening the door to the room, he was greeted by congratulatory shouts from many of his co-workers. His boss then informed him that she had received a promotion to another hotel and that Lee had been selected to take her place. The surprise party was for him. Sue shook Lee's hand, congratulated him on the promotion, and encouraged him to join the celebration. Dazed, Lee was not quite ready to celebrate. His first thoughts were of the increased time commitment the promotion would entail. He asked Sue if they could step out in the hall to discuss the details of the promotion. Lee then told Sue of his surprise about the party and the promotion. Sue responded by saying that she was delighted for Lee, that he was a real asset to the organization, and that she had pushed hard to make this promotion happen. Lee explained that the promotion was "certainly unexpected" and that he was "somewhat hesitant to accept the responsibility."

Sue then briefly outlined the details of the job and reiterated her approval of Lee's work. She told him that there would be both increased responsibility and compensation. Lee then said that he had a few concerns about the promotion. Not wanting her to think that he was unappreciative, he said, "I have thoroughly enjoyed working at the front desk and I'm grateful for everything you and the hotel have done for me, but I'm afraid that taking the position of front office manager will mean less time with my family."

"I understand your concern," she said, "and yes, I admit that the position will require a lot of time at first, but after a while you'll probably only have to work five, maybe ten, more hours than you do now. I can sympathize. I don't get to spend as much time with my family as I'd like either but I'm also committed to my career in this company, which provides a lot of rewards."

Lee attempted to continue to explain his reservations about accepting the job, mildly protesting, "But I haven't even seen the job description. I have no idea how much work it really entails or how much of a raise I will get for the extra time and responsibility."

Frowning, Sue asked pointedly, "Are you saying you don't want the position?"

Lee sensed that the communication process was breaking down. He felt threatened by Sue's defensive attitude and feared that she was drawing inappropriate conclusions. His head pounded with the thought that he was being forced to answer "yes" or "no" about accepting the position when he was in fact uncertain and wanted more information. Attempting to be noncommittal, Lee made the comment, "I'm just not sure that this is the right time to take a position like this." Becoming even more defensive, Sue snapped, "Well, fine. So you want me to cancel the whole party?"

Lee assured her that he did not want the party canceled and instead suggested that they both return and enjoy it but that they also meet on Monday morning to discuss the details of the job. The fact that Lee was willing to return to the party encouraged Sue that he was not rejecting the promotion, but he had made it clear that he was truly concerned about the situation and the welfare of his family. Understanding that the party did not provide an appropriate setting for discussion, and sympathizing with his concerns, Sue agreed that the details could be worked out later. Nonetheless, she had put her own reputation on the line and took Lee's reservations about the job quite personally. They agreed to meet at 9:00 A.M. Monday morning in Sue's office. Stepping back into the room, Sue left Lee with a final comment, "I hope you make the right decision."

1. What went wrong in this incident?
2. What might you predict will happen if Lee turns down the promotion?
3. What could have been done to prevent this from happening?

Part Ten

TRAINING

*It will do no good to get on the right track if you
are going in the wrong direction.*

—UNKNOWN

The hospitality industry has for many years been characterized by a philosophy of coming up through the ranks to achieve a managerial position. One of the difficulties of this approach is that the nature of tasks changes dramatically as one rises through the organizational hierarchy. Low-level supervisors are primarily concerned with managing individual relationships with direct subordinates. Middle management is concerned with managing relationships within and among groups of individuals. Top management is often externally focused with an emphasis on strategy. Training is the vehicle that allows people to move from one level to the next, and if training is lacking or inappropriate, the likelihood of success is diminished.

Like the Greek messenger bearing bad news, when training does not prove effective, it is often the trainer who is blamed. When training fails, however, it is seldom because of those conducting the actual training, but it is due to the lack of adequate preparation and follow-up by the organization itself. It is the responsibility of management to assure that any training program is necessary, appropriate, and successful.

Training is often seen as a way to facilitate change, but it must be recognized that training affects everyone in an organization directly or indirectly. If well done, increased profits, promotions, and new jobs may result. If poorly conducted, there can be many negative effects, such as loss of credibility with employees, decreased performance, and increased conflict. Training may be taken too lightly and, to assure success, it needs to be viewed from a larger perspective as a process designed to increase overall effectiveness.

Training is a four-stage process consisting of assessment, development, implementation, and evaluation. In many organizations these steps are not all given adequate attention, the most common mistake being that training begins and ends with implementation. Certain critical factors must be satisfied at each of these stages of training, and specific questions must be asked to assure that all of these factors are given adequate attention. These questions are short and simple: Why are we doing the training, and will it solve our problem? Who should receive and provide the training? What type of training should we be doing? When should we do the training? Where should the training take place? How can the training be most effective? If these questions are answered thoroughly, it is likely that a successful training experience will follow.

In today's business environment hospitality organizations are seeking to minimize their training expenses by relying more on colleges and universities to prepare students for careers in the industry. For accounting purposes, training is viewed as an expense, but it should also be viewed as an investment in the future of an organization if employees are retained and continue to develop their knowledge and abilities.

Overview of the Incidents

Most of you have received some training in your lives, probably what is commonly referred to as "on-the-job training," which is a haphazard approach at best. Without proper training it is extremely difficult to provide high-quality service. The following scenarios illustrate the outcomes of training efforts in several hospitality organizations.

Case 47

The Swimming Pool

The private Farmingwood Swim & Tennis Club is a midsized club with a membership of 500 families and a full-time staff of 20 people. The club has a variety of facilities, including two pools, 10 tennis courts, an exercise room, a full-service dining room, and seven acres of landscaped property. The general manager of the club is ultimately responsible for the routine maintenance and repair of the facilities, and she assigns daily tasks to a single maintenance engineer. The maintenance engineer is required to have a working knowledge of electrical repair, basic plumbing, painting, light construction, and pool maintenance.

In December 1993, the manager of the club fired the maintenance engineer who had been with the property for over five years. After a three-week recruitment period, the manager hired a new maintenance engineer, Mr. Angelo. He was the most qualified applicant for the position, as he had spent the past 20 years as a licensed contractor in the area. Mr. Angelo was proficient in all of the necessary areas but had a limited knowledge of pool repair and maintenance. The general manager believed that Mr. Angelo's experience as a licensed contractor would compensate for his limited knowledge about pools and that his participation in a four-day "pool school" training program would provide him with the additional knowledge that he would need for the position.

After a three-day orientation at the club, Mr. Angelo began regular duties as the maintenance engineer. The assistant manager of the club provided Mr. Angelo with the technical support that he needed until he was proficient with the assigned tasks and was capable of working independently. The assistant manager told the general manager that while Mr. Angelo was performing all of the assigned duties skillfully, enrollment in a four-day pool school was still necessary.

During the next three weeks, Mr. Angelo impressed the general manager with his reliability and task performance. At this point, activity at the club was steadily increasing, and the general manager believed that she could not afford to send Mr. Angelo to the pool school program. At this time she believed that the maintenance and repair of the pool simply required the application of basic electrical and plumbing skills and that he could handle any problems associated with the pool. Further, she believed that if a major problem did occur, she could easily hire a professional pool contractor to solve the problem.

On Friday, March 19, disaster struck. Mr. Angelo arrived at the club at 9:00 A.M., he walked through the clubhouse, then went downstairs to check the pool and the grounds. Upon arriving at the pool, Mr. Angelo was met by three club members with red, swollen eyes and severely damaged bathing suits. The members angrily interrogated Mr. Angelo about the chemical balance of the water in the pool, claiming that something was terribly wrong. Mr. Angelo apologized to the members and promised that he would check the chemical balance and report back to them immediately. Upon reaching the pool pumphouse, Mr. Angelo discovered that the chlorine pump was delivering chlorine to the pool at an abnormally high rate. He noticed further that the chlorine tank, which had been filled to the 250-gallon mark the previous day, was far below the 150-gallon mark.

To understand the magnitude of the problem, some technical information may be useful. The optimum level of chlorine in a public swimming pool is 1.5 parts of chlorine per 1 million parts of water. It takes approximately 10 gallons of chlorine to raise a 218,000-gallon pool by 1 part per million. Thus the 100 gallons or more of chlorine that had entered the pool raised the chlorine/water ratio to almost 10 times the optimum amount. Chlorine, a compound similar to household bleach, is a virulent chemical that is dangerous to human beings in high concentrations. Similar to household bleach, chlorine irritates mucous membranes and damages the synthetic fibers found in clothing. Those members who had spent time in the pool during the overchlorination experienced irritations to their eyes, noses, throats, and lungs. In addition, the high concentration of chlorine had removed color from bathing suits in some cases and ruined completely the material in others.

After discovering the dangerous chemical imbalance in the pool, Mr. Angelo immediately approached the members who had complained initially. Mr. Angelo explained that some type of computer failure had occurred during the night, allowing the chlorine pump to deliver chlorine to the pool without automatic monitoring. Mr. Angelo offered a sincere apology for the problem and assured members that the pool would be returned to the proper chemical balance by evening. Although the members understood Mr. Angelo's explanation of the cause of the incident, they were still upset about their bathing suits and their physical health. Faced with a problem that was both technical and guest service related, neither of which he knew how to resolve, Mr. Angelo became quite defensive in the conversation that ensued with the injured guests. Mr. Angelo's attitude infuriated the members and prompted them to approach the general manager regarding her ability to manage the club.

When the general manager was informed of the problem, she immediately called a professional pool contractor to determine its cause. The contractor examined the pool pumphouse and determined that the overchlorination had been caused by a valve that was left in the open position accidentally. In fact, Mr. Angelo had refilled the chlorine tank on Thursday morning and had performed the task based on his memory of being shown the procedure once without fully understanding what he was doing. Pool operations were restored to normal within a period of three hours, and club members were allowed to enter the pool safely at this time.

Mr. Angelo was very troubled as a result of the incident. First, he felt a deep sense of compassion for the members who were standing before him with irritated eyes, noses, throats, and lungs. His response was to offer sincere apologies and to assure members that the problem would be resolved as soon as possible. Unfortunately, Mr. Angelo felt unable to promise that the problem would never occur again, due to his lack of understanding of pool maintenance and repair. Second, Mr. Angelo felt anxious about his continued employment at the club. Considering that he was still a relatively new employee, he feared that such a major disaster might cause him to be fired. To protect himself, Mr. Angelo made it extremely clear to the members that the overchlorination occurred due to a computer failure and not a human error. Mr. Angelo felt compelled to make this claim even though he was not sure about the true cause of the incident. Third, Mr. Angelo felt anger toward the general manager for placing him in these difficult circumstances.

1. Was Mr. Angelo qualified for the position of maintenance engineer?
2. Evaluate the training that Mr. Angelo received?
3. Compare the long- and short-term costs that might be associated with this incident?

Case 48

The Mystery Guest

Stephen is a 24-year-old graduate of a Colorado university with a bachelor's degree in hospitality management. He has been working at the Boulderado Hotel in Denver for two years and is currently the evening front desk supervisor. The general manager of the Boulderado has a very relaxed attitude and takes policies and formal procedures lightly. For the past year Stephen has been responsible for training new front desk clerks. Training at this property consists of learning where to "punch in," being told when to take meal breaks, and receiving a 15-minute tutorial of the computer system used for checking guests in and out. The rest of the training was quite literally "on the job," where new front desk clerks learned by trial and error.

Late in the summer of Stephen's second year, it was learned that a service quality test was to be conducted at the hotel. The hotel's corporate office would be sending a "mystery guest," who would be appraising the performance of the Boulderado. Although the corporate investigator was supposed to be anonymous, through the grapevine all employees knew the guest's name and time of his arrival well in advance. All the departments were prepared to provide VIP treatment for this guest to ensure a high rating of service quality. The housekeeping department made up his room meticulously, and it was checked by the executive housekeeper and the general manager. Public areas were cleaned completely, and maintenance engineers checked and double-checked all electrical and mechanical systems as well as the physical structure of the building. The kitchens were scoured from top to bottom. For three days prior to his arrival, the hotel worked to achieve perfection for the corporate representative.

On the day of "mystery guest's" arrival, Stephen started his shift at 3 P.M. and was promptly called into the front desk manager's office.

Stephen was told exactly when the corporate guest would arrive and that he was to conduct the check-in to ensure that no faults or mistakes would be made. The front desk manager then gave Stephen a copy of the standardized corporate procedures for checking in a guest. There were specific phrases that a front desk clerk was to use and certain pieces of information that the guest had to be told during check-in. Stephen was told to memorize these phrases and prepare the front desk area for the corporate guest's arrival. He was also instructed to notify other departments as soon as the guest had checked in.

The front desk crew waited for the corporate representative to arrive, and when he did, Stephen stepped toward him and repeated the procedurally correct greeting he had learned an hour before. However, after the formal greeting and an initial attempt to follow the corporate procedures, Stephen lapsed into his own check-in system, which he had developed into a comfortable yet efficient routine over the past two years. The corporate phrases were forgotten, as was mentioning the location of ice machines, the hotel restaurant, and the lounge. Having his routine disrupted by the new procedures, Stephen additionally neglected to explain the complimentary cocktail hour and continental breakfast. The guest had to ask many questions in order to receive the basic information that Stephen usually explains when comfortably using his own methods and procedures. Finally, the guest was checked in, pertinent information was conveyed, and Stephen was able to relax again.

Three weeks later Stephen was called into the front desk manager's office to discuss the results of the analysis. Among others, one of the major problems was the check-in process. Stephen was verbally reprimanded for not following procedures and was told that his chances for advancement had decreased considerably. Stephen attempted to explain that his training had come two years too late and he questioned why his performance was not evaluated and changed during the previous two years if it was not consistent with corporate specifications. Stephen was also angry that he had been asked to learn standardized procedures three hours before the analyst was to arrive and to change his well-established routine at the last minute. Although the front desk manager could not provide adequate answers, he was firm in his reproach of Stephen. Stephen left the office defeated and wondering what was the point of continuing to work hard if his promotion opportunities were lost because he had not been trained correctly to do his job.

1. Is Stephen at fault here? Why or why not?
2. Discuss the pros and cons of a strictly controlled check-in procedure.
3. Do you think that this type of corporate assessment is effective?

Case 49

The Apprentice Chef

Benno Schatz, a native German in his early thirties, decided to make a career change. Although he studied history and art for six years, he had a fascination with cooking. Having always enjoyed working with food and creating new recipes, he decided to train to become a chef. Shortly after making this decision, he was hired as an apprentice chef by a recently opened hotel in the city of Cologne that is a member of a major international chain. Benno realized that learning the skills of his new profession would be a challenge, but he was determined to work hard and was committed to succeed as a chef.

The following year he entered a two-year chef's training program that had just been established by the hotel in conjunction with an independent local culinary school. Benno was the first employee to participate in this program. He worked four days a week in the hotel and he attended class once a week. The program was unique in its structure, as it relied heavily on Benno's work in the hotel kitchen as an apprentice to the executive chef, to provide a significant portion of his training. As part of the arrangement with the culinary school, the hotel had agreed to teach Benno to prepare approximately 300 dishes. Upon completing the program he would receive the "qualified chef" degree, which is recognized as an important culinary certification in Germany.

Two months before Benno was to complete the program, the school sent a list of dishes to the executive chef of the hotel, asking whether Benno was familiar with the 300 meals or whether there was some need for further training. They added that he might be asked to prepare any one of these dishes as part of his final exam. The executive chef responded to the school, writing that his trainee was familiar with each of the dishes. He did not inform Benno about the correspondence.

By chance, Benno learned about the list and the executive chef's response from one of his instructors at school. He looked through the list and realized that there were a great number of dishes that he did not know how to prepare. Benno wondered how the executive chef could have given such a response without first speaking with him. He concluded that the executive chef did not really care about him and his training program; otherwise, they would have reviewed the list together, identified the gaps in his knowledge, and worked to fill them. Benno was very disappointed in the executive chef's behavior and his apparent disregard for his apprentice. Nonetheless, Benno was concerned about passing his final exam and decided to let the executive chef know that he was not familiar with all of the dishes on the list. He left a note in the chef's mailbox with the names of those meals in which he would need further training.

The next day Benno was summoned to come to the chef's office immediately. The executive chef was outraged at his trainee's lack of knowledge. He told Benno that if he was not able to prepare these "simple" dishes after almost two years of training, it would be best for him to stay on as a trainee for another six months to learn to prepare them. He added that it would be of no use to argue about his decision and told Benno to leave the office.

Benno wanted under no circumstances to stay another six months as a trainee because the salary was much lower than that of a certified chef. By the end of the day, Benno was able to persuade the executive chef not to extend the period of training. The executive chef agreed that he might graduate on time, but on the condition that he was to study for himself the preparation of the meals with which he had no experience. Benno agreed to the terms and worked very hard independently to master the unfamiliar recipes. He graduated from the program on time two months after the incident and soon left to work for another hotel in Cologne. Today he is a well-known chef in the city.

1. Evaluate the training program in which Benno was enrolled.
2. Were the demands made on Benno reasonable?
3. Discuss the attitude and behavior of the executive chef.

Case 50

Bongo's

Ramon Manuel was a manager with Bongo's, a large national chain of casual theme restaurants that operates at over 150 locations. Bongo's is owned by a larger restaurant conglomeration which operates three additional restaurant concepts and an on-site food and beverage management company. The Bongo's chain is well established, but there is a very high level of management turnover in the organization.

At 37, Ramon had worked in various independent restaurants for 15 years prior to being hired by Bongo's. Even with his experience he knew that he would be required to complete Bongo's management training program. Managers at Bongo's are proud of the fact that they are "hands-on" managers. Ramon began his management training program, as did all other managers at the company, with a brief orientation conducted by the area director, followed by an overview of the entire training program which he was told would take an average of approximately nine months.

Following the day of orientation, Ramon began his official training program as a prep cook in the kitchen of the restaurant to which he had been assigned. After achieving the required level of proficiency in this position, he moved on to the dish room, the grill, the fry station, and the pantry. Ramon started to become restless after working in the kitchen for over four weeks and having developed more than the required proficiency in all positions. By this time he had expected to be moved to the front of the house for his hourly training but was told that he would need to stay in the kitchen a bit longer to "help out." His goal was to master the hourly job function of his training as quickly as possible, both to receive the increase in salary that the completion of this portion of training entails and to begin working actual management shifts at the restaurant.

Ramon suspected that he was being used by the company as a labor-saving tool by being kept in the kitchen for such a significant amount of time. He was aware that other managers and management trainees were also spending long hours in the kitchen, presumably to save on labor cost. With a little investigative work, Ramon learned that the company operated on a very tight budget. For each outlet to meet the company's financial expectations and unit performance, it was not at all unusual for managers and management trainees to be used in place of hourly employees to minimize additional labor costs. Although he remembered the company's pride in its hands-on managers, he wasn't sure he agreed with this approach.

After approximately eight weeks in the kitchen, Ramon was finally able to speak with the area director and to have the kitchen training modules tested and signed off. At this time differences were already arising among Ramon, the general manager, and the area director concerning the training program and the role of management in the organization. When Ramon had begun with the company he had been assured by the area director that because of his experience, he would move rapidly through the hourly portion of the training program. As it became obvious to Ramon that his training time expectations were not going to be met, he became discouraged and angry at both the company and its managers. He began to reconsider his decision to work with Bongo's, as he continued to feel that the restaurant was taking advantage of the management trainees to meet tight labor budgets.

With these thoughts on his mind, Ramon worked through hourly training in the front of house with a visibly lower level of enthusiasm and productivity as well as a reduced overall commitment to the company. Realizing Ramon's discouragement with the training process and not wanting to lose another potential manager, the general manager and the area director then rushed him through the rest of the hourly training program. The change in the attitude of the general manager and the area director was disconcerting to Ramon, as he realized that it came only after he vocalized his dissatisfaction. Ramon was increasingly aware that the culture of the chain regarding management style was not consistent with his beliefs. Not only did Ramon feel that using managers and management trainees to cover hourly positions created morale problems, he also believed that it minimized the credibility of the managers in the eyes of the employees they were to supervise, thereby reducing their ability to manage those subordinates effectively. Once an energetic and promising new manager, Ramon left the company after only five months and accepted a management position with a competing restaurant.

1. Evaluate Bongo's training program.
2. Should everyone be put through the same training? Why or why not?
3. What are some of the relationships between training and turnover?

Part Eleven

REWARD SYSTEMS

Behavior that gets rewarded gets repeated.
—B. F. SKINNER

If you ask a group of hospitality managers how many want to know when their performance is not meeting their manager's expectations, virtually all of them will raise their hand. If you then ask this same group how many of them feel comfortable giving their subordinates negative feedback, virtually none of them will raise their hand. It is this inconsistency that creates major problems for employees and results in tremendous anxiety for both managers and subordinates when it comes time for annual performance reviews.

Reward systems are often viewed strictly in terms of monetary compensation but in fact are more complex than that. They are comprised of daily feedback, formal performance reviews, the work itself, as well as the wage or salary a person may receive for his or her work. What is perceived as a reward may vary from person to person. A day off without pay may be appreciated by a single person with a busy social calendar but for the head of a large family the lost income may mean that the children may not eat as well that week. It is important to recognize which rewards are valued by employees.

Rewards come in two primary forms, extrinsic and intrinsic. Extrinsic rewards come from the organization in the form of wages, benefits, promotions, and performance reviews. Instrinic rewards come from the work itself if tasks are interesting, challenging, and have an impact on others. The manager has a lot of control over the design of systems to provide rewards for his or her subordinates, but often does not capitalize on the opportunity. To be motivating to employees, extrinsic rewards must be linked to performance. Praise from the manager following an employee's effective handling of a guest complaint is a good example. To be intrinsically rewarding, work must be structured to be meaningful for employees. Encouraging contact with guests, job rotation, and work teams are ways to accomplish this.

Performance appraisals serve two primary functions: to determine merit increases and to provide task-related feedback. No employee should ever be surprised during an annual performance review because the manager should be continually providing feedback, both positive and negative, contingent on the employee's performance.

To be effective in motivating employees, compensation must be linked to performance. For some positions, such as waitstaff, this relationship is obvious. For many positions, however, a manager must be creative to establish these links. Profit-sharing or incentive systems are ways that this can be accomplished. Verbal praise or recognition programs can also act as powerful rewards.

It is important that managers be aware of the behaviors that are being rewarded. For example, managers occasionally develop reward systems that create excessive competition among employees. If a manager wants to encourage people to work together a system of group rewards might be appropriate.

For managers to maximize their effectiveness, they need to understand reward systems in a broader context. Rewards must be valued by employees and must be administered contingent on employee performance. Rewards can come in many forms, such as praising, mentoring, participating in decisions, or redesigning a task. Even a dishwasher can be made to feel important if the job is viewed as important by the supervisor, to fellow employees, and to guests.

Overview of the Incidents

The following scenarios describe reward systems that were thoughtfully designed, but perhaps did not work out exactly as planned. Those who are being rewarded ultimately determine whether or not a reward system is effective.

Case 51

The University Conference Center

Laura Morton had worked at the University Conference Center for a month and a half as a front desk clerk. Previously, she had spent several years working in retail, some of that time in a managerial capacity. She left the retail industry because she no longer enjoyed it. In accepting the position at the Conference Center, she knew she would be starting at the bottom as she had no previous hotel experience, but hoped eventually to establish a long-term career in the industry. During her first six weeks, she had learned a substantial amount about the operation of the front desk, including the computer system, reservations, and concierge. She had picked it all up very quickly, and within this brief period of time felt completely comfortable in her new position. In addition, she seemed to have the confidence of the front office manager, Nick.

After Laura had been employed for nearly two months, one of three supervisors was promoted to another department and a new supervisor had not yet been hired. By dividing the extra work between the other remaining supervisor and himself, Nick could cover all the shifts during the week except for Tuesday and Thursday evenings. Nick was in a difficult situation, already overworked, and not wanting to cover the extra Tuesday and Thursday shifts for an extended period of time. The possibility of promoting Laura had been considered, but company policy prohibited anyone from being promoted prior to 90 days from the date of hire, since that was the term of the required probationary period.

To deal with the situation, Nick decided that Laura could be acting supervisor on Tuesday and Thursday. She would be in charge of closing the shift and dealing with any problems or guest complaints that might come up. Laura was excited about the opportunity for greater responsibility and was pleased with the confidence that Nick showed in her. She did not mind that she would not receive the $1.05/hour raise that would come with the promotion, since she was only doing it twice a week for a few weeks, and she felt confident that with this experience she would get the promotion following her probationary period.

Over the course of the next two weeks, Laura had four supervisory shifts. Two of the four were very quiet, while the other two were very busy. Because she was not yet completely familiar with the closing procedure for the shift, she had to stay somewhat longer than scheduled to finish her paperwork, especially on the one day that there were a large number of checkouts.

One evening at the end of the two-week period, Laura came home from the movies to discover a message from Nick on her answering machine. Over the past week she had stayed at work too long on two occasions. In an effort to cut down on overtime, Nick asked that she come to work two hours late the next day so that she would not exceed 40 hours for the week. Any time worked over 40 hours was paid at time and a half, and Nick was under pressure from upper management to minimize any overtime expenses for front office clerks. She would also have to come to his office to get her time card that next morning because Nick had pulled it out from its normal place among the rest of the time cards.

Laura was furious. Not only had Nick's "request" been left on the answering machine with little notice for her to change her transportation plans for the next morning, but she felt Nick was taking advantage of her. She was doing a supervisor's job at a regular clerk's wage rate, and the only overtime she had was on the shifts for which she was supervisor. Laura fumed for awhile before calming down and thinking clearly. She did not want to fly off the handle at Nick because there was more at stake than the short-term pay; she wanted the promotion to supervisor. The last thing she wanted in her file was a note about an argument with her manager, but she was not going to let herself be taken advantage of by the hotel.

The next day, she went in to work only an hour late so that she could talk to Nick ahead of time. She explained her feelings clearly and carefully, emphasizing that the only time she had worked overtime was during the supervisory shifts. She said she understood his position and hoped he understood hers. Much to her surprise, he did. He simply said that he would pay her an extra $25 per week out of petty cash as a "miscellaneous expense" for the remaining weeks that she would be supervisor. In return, however, she had to keep overtime down by punching out after 40 hours even if she had to work a few hours longer. Laura went away feeling that Nick had listened to her complaint and acted in a manner that benefited both parties. Nick felt that he had made an excellent managerial decision that resolved his problem.

1. Does the promotion policy make sense? Why or why not?
2. Was Nick's decision "excellent," as he believed?

Case 52

The Greek Palace

The Greek Palace Hotel is located just outside Olympia, the site of the ancient Olympic games. The hotel is one of 110 located around all of Greece that is owned by the Greek Tourism Organization (EOT), a government enterprise. The Greek government will contract for the management of these hotels to the highest bidders, regardless of hospitality experience or managerial knowledge. The contract specifies that the Greek government will receive 20 percent of the gross profit and will provide funding for marketing, allowing affiliated hotels to advertise through their tourism bureaus in Europe. The Greek government will often continue to fund these hotels, even if losses are incurred, in order to expand the tourism market.

The accepted wage structure for privately owned businesses in Greece is that most waiters and bartenders are paid a percentage of the profits, which they split equally at the end of the shift. This percentage is built into the price charged to customers and the customers are aware of this fact, so tipping is not customary. In the government-owned sector of the hotel industry, the labor laws are different, a fact about which most customers are unaware. Employees are paid a basic wage with no tips and often work long shifts.

Dimitri had just driven to Olympia from Sparta, a three-hour drive through the mountainous terrain of the Peloponnese. He had arrived late in the evening and checked into his room at the Greek Palace Hotel without any problem. Since it was a beautiful night he decided to have a drink at the outdoor cafe situated around the hotel pool. Dimitri could hear a commotion from the bar across the pool, and as no wait staff were in sight, he seated himself, opting for a table designed for four after noting that all the tables for two were occupied.

A waiter arrived at his table about 15 minutes later and asked him if he could possibly find a seat at the bar to leave some room for any arriving groups of customers. Dimitri saw that several of the tables had been vacated and that, if needed, the wait staff could clear those tables to seat any new customers. After a brief discussion, the waiter conceded to Dimitri and allowed him to sit at the table of his choice. The waiter took Dimitri's order and quickly returned to the bar to place the order. Dimitri could see that the wait staff and bartenders were swamped with beverage and food orders and realized that he might not get his drink quickly, especially after his little confrontation with the waiter. The cafe seemed to be understaffed, two waiters and two bartenders, for well over 100 people. He could not see into the kitchen, but he could easily see the bar from across the pool. One of the bartenders had been relegated to the back of the bar to make ice cream sundaes and toasts.

Finally, after 20 minutes Dimitri was served his drink. The waiter simply put the drink down and left the table without saying a word to him. Before Dimitri could ask for some nuts and hors d'oeuvres, traditionally provided with a cocktail in Greece, the waiter frantically ran back to the bar, where another order was ready to be served.

The next time the waiter came by, Dimitri asked him for some peanuts and cashews to go along with his drink. The waiter said that he was too busy to bother with such details. Dimitri was slightly riled with the tone of voice the waiter had used and asked to see the manager of the hotel. Ten minutes later, the manager of the hotel came to Dimitri's table and apologized for the incident, citing a lack of personnel for the problems. Dimitri did eventually get his hors d'oeuvres, but service continued to be slow and unfriendly.

After a second drink, Dimitri departed to his room for the night and awoke in the morning to get ready to travel to Patra. As he was seated in the cafe to have his morning coffee, he was shocked to see that there were five people working the morning shift at the outdoor cafe although there were only a handful of customers to be served. He had seen all five of them sitting around the bar having drinks while chaos was reigning the previous night. Dimitri paid his bill and departed, promising never to visit this hotel again.

1. What impact did the compensation system have on employee behavior?
2. What else was wrong in this situation?

Case 53

The New Sales Manager

Chris Barlow is a sales manager at a downtown convention hotel, The Rio Grande, in Dallas, Texas. Although he had previous experience in the banquet division of another hotel, Chris is an absolute newcomer to sales. He was hired six months ago by the director of sales, Bob Norton, who felt Chris had sales potential. Company policy required a low starting salary, during what Bob referred to as a "training phase," but he assured Chris that within a short time he would be "up to speed" and eligible for up to a 25 percent raise. He was told that people who hold director of sales positions all over the city began their careers in the very same position as Chris. Anticipating a higher salary eventually in the sales position and greater career opportunities, Chris was persuaded to leave his banquet job, taking a significant pay cut. He made a commitment to himself to complete his training as efficiently and effectively as possible.

During his interview and throughout the first few weeks of his employment, Chris was promised "excellent training." He anticipated that this would be a set program of a specific duration during which he would be given practice exercises regarding the department's paperwork and computer procedures as well as specific language to use in making sales calls. However, after having worked at the Rio Grande for over two months, the extent of his training consisted of following Bob, the director of sales, to Austin so that Chris could meet a couple of his business contacts. On his own initiative, Chris read a sales training manual from another hotel that he borrowed from a friend and he made a few cold calls. By constantly asking the other sales managers questions, Chris tried to learn the business as best as he could.

As an employee of the Rio Grande, Chris is diligent and he willingly works extra time when it's needed, particularly to learn a new skill or to "go the extra mile" in his job. He does not see his job as a daily task but as a challenging, exciting, and ongoing project in which his performance directly affects the hotel's success. In return he expects the management of the Rio Grande to have a similar commitment to the sales staff, particularly in providing the training and resources they need to perform their jobs. Quickly, Chris found that his co-workers in the sales department have a vastly different view of their positions. The other four sales managers see their jobs as a 9-to-5 experience which keeps them busy and pays their bills. They see no benefit in working longer hours, participating in formalized training, or securing greater sales, as the hotel does not pay any commissions or bonuses. Their raises are awarded based on daily activity, specifically the number of phone calls made during the day and not the amount of business that they bring to the hotel.

Although Chris became a competent sales manager in a relatively short period of time, he keeps thinking about the fact that he has still not received the formal training he expected. The most compelling problem to Chris is that the sales staff at the hotel, including his supervisor, are not working to make anything better. He feels that with some guidance from either the director of sales or a senior sales manager he could become an even more effective salesperson. No one even suggested that he learn more about the hotel beyond his two-night "training stay."

Within his first three months, Chris booked over 50 room nights with seven clients, all of whom were solicited solely by Chris. He felt with continued performance at this level that he would secure the promised salary increase. Bob had recently informed the sales office that the following week was going to be a sales blitz for the department and that they should expect to be out of the office all day, making calls on new prospective customers. Chris had already scheduled a meeting for that week, but he decided that he could call and shorten the meeting to the hour between 12:30 P.M. and 1:30 P.M. when he knew that the sales blitz would be interrupted for lunch. He really wanted this potential customer to see the hotel and eat in the restaurant to show him the quality of the service that the Rio Grande had to offer.

When his co-workers discovered that he intended to keep the appointment during the sales blitz week, they accused him of being insubordinate and berated him for "showing off" by doing more than the expected work. He was told that he could not make appointments that week with anyone he had contacted previously because the sales blitz was designed to focus exclusively on establishing *new* contacts in the area. Chris wanted to respond to their comments, specifically to question the logic of not meeting a prospective customer, but decided against raising the issue. Chris knew that an argument with his co-workers about the blitz week would only increase the tension that was developing toward him. Their invitations to play golf had ceased, and they were now beginning to ignore him in the office. At the same time, he felt terribly frustrated that the other sales managers not only seemed indifferent about generating business for the hotel but that they resented his efforts to do so.

Feeling at a loss within his own department, Chris decided to approach the general manager with his concerns. He suggested the idea of putting the sales managers on some sort of goal-oriented commission, plus a base salary, to boost their enthusiasm and production in their jobs.

His meeting with the general manager was very discouraging and revealed to Chris why Bob, the current director of sales, did not attempt to spark enthusiasm in the sales department. The general manager believed that as long as the sales managers were "spreading the word" about the hotel, the name brand itself would bring in most of the business. The GM did not feel that utilizing an incentive system, such as commissions or bonuses, would in any way benefit the hotel and that instead it would cause turnover in the sales department. Left at a dead end, Chris knew that he had no choice but to call the prospective customer and reschedule the luncheon meeting.

1. As an internal customer, were Chris's expectations met?
2. What caused the behavior of his peers and his manager?
3. What advice might you give to Chris?
4. How would you operate the department, given the attitude of the general manager?

Case 54

The Incentive System

Cindy Spence is the front office manager of a four-star hotel in Jacksonville, Florida. She had recently attended a three-day management training seminar in Miami and returned to her job full of ideas about how to improve service at the front desk. The one concept that really stuck in her mind was the importance of linking performance to rewards. The instructor had told the class several times that "behavior that gets rewarded gets repeated."

In the monthly rooms division meeting, guest comment cards that have been returned from the corporate office are reviewed. Last month it seemed that there were several complaints about the time it took to check in or out of the hotel. This really bothered Cindy and she wanted to reduce the number of complaints about her department. To do so, she decided to put to work the knowledge she had obtained at the management seminar. She devised a system that would reward the front office personnel for providing fast service.

Cindy told her subordinates about the guest comment cards and her resulting disappointment at the next department meeting, where she also introduced her new program. "It is quite simple, really," she explained, "the two people who check in the most guests and check out the most guests during an eight-hour shift will receive a bonus at the end of the month." The system seemed to work beautifully, and she rewarded two employees with $50 bills on the first day of the following month. The next month things continued to go quite well, and the lines really did move along more quickly than they had in the past. It did not seem as though her staff was as friendly or helpful to each other as they had been in the past, but overall, Cindy was delighted with her success.

At the monthly rooms division meeting, Cindy's enthusiasm waned considerably, however. It seems that while incoming and outgoing guests were moving through the system much more quickly, they were now complaining about the lack of friendliness and courtesy from the front desk personnel. One guest commented, "I felt like I was a steer being herded into the corral. This is *not* the type of service I expect from a hotel of this caliber." Cindy was very perplexed and expressed her frustration, "They want speed and they want courtesy, how can we do both?" Her troubles were just beginning, however, as the controller began to describe the errors that had been made in the posting of accounts. In an effort to speed up the checkout procedure, many charges were not being posted to the bill, resulting in errors and lost revenue. Similarly, necessary information was not being entered into the computer system upon check-in, making the issuing of statements much more difficult. It had been necessary on many occasions to try to find guests' home addresses in telephone books so that a bill could be sent to them. In several instances the controller was not even sure if the bills were being sent to the right person. Cindy was quickly losing her faith in theories of management.

1. What is wrong with Cindy's incentive system?
2. Should she lose her faith in theories of management?

Case 55

The River Walk Cafe

The River Walk Cafe is a casual, 250-seat restaurant located in downtown San Antonio, Texas. The cafe serves three meals and has a brisk bar business at night. Although there are some slow periods during the year, business is steady due to a loyal local customer base, and a constant supply of tourist and convention customers.

The general manager is Gary MacAfee. He's been with the cafe a little over six months. The previous general manager left for another business opportunity. After finishing his undergraduate degree in business administration, Gary spent seven years working his way up the front-of-house and back-of-house management ranks in a large national restaurant chain. This is his first general manager position.

Gary took a very conservative approach when he began his new position. He knew he could improve the overall quality of operations and increase revenues. However, he also knew that if he acted too quickly and made a lot of changes early on, his staff and customers may be resentful and resist.

The first item on Gary's agenda was get a sense of the cafe's operating procedures and general work climate. To do this, Gary worked directly with the kitchen and wait staffs, performing the same tasks, duties, and responsibilities that they performed. He felt it was important to gain the employees' respect by showing that he wasn't afraid to get his hands dirty. In addition, Gary would learn firsthand about the cafe's operations. He also started a file that contained a log of customer and staff comments, interactions among the staff and customers, sales and revenue figures, and any information he could use to gain a comprehensive understanding of the current working conditions and use subsequently as a basis for making necessary changes.

After a couple of months, Gary had compiled a long list of items he thought he could use as a basis for improvement.

One of Gary's biggest concerns was the relationship between the kitchen staff and the wait staff. He recorded numerous problems and tensions. To begin, Gary noticed that the servers spent a great deal of time interacting intensively with the guests. However, he also noticed that the wait staff were quite terse and demanding of the kitchen staff. Servers complained that it took too long for food to come out because the cooks wasted their time garnishing plates. However, the cooks complained that many times the food waited too long on the hot counter and "died" before it was picked up by the wait staff because the waiters and waitresses were "schmoozing" with the customers. Gary also found that when the wait staff did occasionally bus tables, they returned the dish and glass trays without stacking them in their proper places. The kitchen staff complained bitterly, noting that the kitchen was crowded enough without trays of dishes and glassware carelessly stacked in valuable prep space.

To address this problem, Gary decided to conduct a meeting with the wait staff and inform them of his findings. Gary felt that it was appropriate to discuss his concerns with the front-of-house employees first, then determine how to involve the back-of-house employees. Initially, the meeting was not very insightful. Needless to say, the wait staff were not happy about being told of Gary's "perceived problems" with the operations. In fact, they felt that he was pointing the finger at them. As such, they did not provide Gary with much information to identify the true nature of the problems, let alone determine ways of making the situation better.

However, when Gary asked the wait staff about their satisfaction with specific aspects of work, particularly pay, they became very vocal. Sarah, a full-timer who had been with the cafe for two years, stated that in comparison to other waiters and waitresses in the area, the cafe wait staff made considerably less. As the discussion ensued, it became clear that this issue was a really big sore spot among all of the wait staff. They suggested that the primary problem was that the River Walk Cafe is one of only two casual restaurants in the downtown convention district. Because most of the other restaurants are upscale, the wait staff at the other establishments earn considerably more in tips because they have higher check totals.

Sarah also affirmed Gary's observation concerning the "extensive" time spent with customers and stated that the wait staff felt it was important to "get to know your table." However, Sarah said that the time is necessary in order to upsell the guest to increase the check total. Steve, a part-time server, concurred: "It's important to understand your customers. If we didn't spend as much time as we do, we couldn't provide the kind of service they expect. Besides, upselling and providing good service makes you happy and brings the customers back. Isn't that what you want?"

After much thought and consideration, Gary decided it was necessary to revise the compensation system for the wait staff. He felt that it was necessary to provide some additional monetary incentives for the wait staff, but not at the expense of the cafe's overall profitability. The new system must provide a mechanism for increasing the cafe's overall revenues. In addition, the wait staff must take on some additional responsibilities so that the kitchen staff could accommodate the need for an increase in table service efficiency. As such, the wait staff were required to garnish their own plates and bus their own tables.

Gary increased the wait staff's base wage 25 percent, from $2.90 an hour to $3.60 an hour. In addition, he developed incentives for outstanding individual and group performance. Free end-of-shift meals would be awarded to the waiter or waitress who turned the most tables, and to the person who had the highest sales for the shift. In addition, the entire wait staff would receive a biweekly bonus if the cafe's overall sales reached specified levels. Gary felt that this new system would alleviate the pay-inequity problem and promote a more cohesive, motivated front-of-house staff. Moreover, Gary believed that this new system would have a positive impact on the bottom line.

The wait staff were very pleased with the new system. They openly expressed their appreciation about receiving a wage increase. In addition, they realized that they didn't have to "schmooze" with the guests to increase their individual and overall sales—simply turning more tables by providing more efficient service had a positive net result. Finally, the wait staff seemed to enjoy their new responsibilities, and they even had informal contests to see who could come up with the most creative garnishing designs.

However, while the wait staff were happy with the new system, the kitchen staff expressed a great deal of anger and resentment. The kitchen staff felt betrayed. Henry, one of the line cooks, summed it up by stating, "We work just as hard as they do, but you've ignored our efforts. It's not fair!" Gary realized that his new system had perhaps created more problems than it solved.

1. Did Gary's new incentive system solve his primary problem?
2. Will it help the cafe achieve its goal of high-quality customer service?
3. What advice might you have for Gary?